SCOTTISH EMPIRE

Scots in pursuit of Hope and Glory

Helen Smailes

SCOTTISH NATIONAL PORTRAIT GALLERY

EDINBURGH
HER MAJESTY'S STATIONERY OFFICE

Designed by HMSO Graphic Design/Edinburgh

ISBN 0 11 491743 4

Front cover Colonel Alexander Gardner

Back cover David Livingstone

CONTENTS

ACKNOWLEDGEMENTS

Scottish Empire is based on an experimental display which was arranged by the Scottish National Portrait Gallery in 1980 and for which most of the exhibits were drawn from the Gallery's own permanent collection.

I am grateful to all other public galleries and private owners who have kindly allowed me to illustrate items from their collections and to the following for help and information: the Graphics Group of the Scottish Development Department; the National Library of Scotland; the Scottish Record Office; the National Portrait Gallery, London; Mrs M Butt of New College Library, Edinburgh; Miss Dale Idiens of the Royal Scottish Museum; the Right Honourable the Earl of Leven and Melville.

I am particularly indebted to all my colleagues for their constant support and encouragement and to Mrs Helen Sharp for her typing.

Helen Smailes
February 1981

'We call ourselves insular, but the truth is that we are the only race on earth that can produce men capable of getting inside the skins of remote people. Perhaps the Scots are better than the English, but we're all a thousand per cent better than anybody else.'

John Buchan Greenmantle

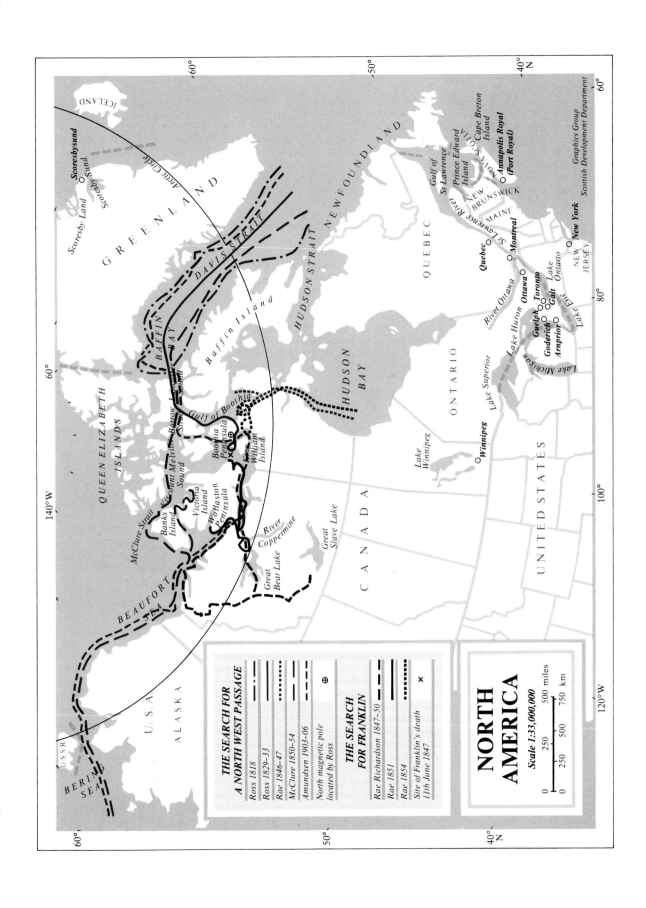

THE SEARCH FOR
A NORTH WEST PASSAGE

Ross 1818
Ross 1829–33
Rae 1846–47
McClure 1850–54
Amundsen 1903–06
North magnetic pole ⊕
located by Ross

THE SEARCH
FOR FRANKLIN

Rae Richardson 1847–50
Rae 1851
Rae 1854
Site of Franklin's death ✕
11th June 1847

NORTH
AMERICA

Scale 1:33,000,000

0   250   500 miles
0 250 500 750 km

Graphics Group
Scottish Development Department

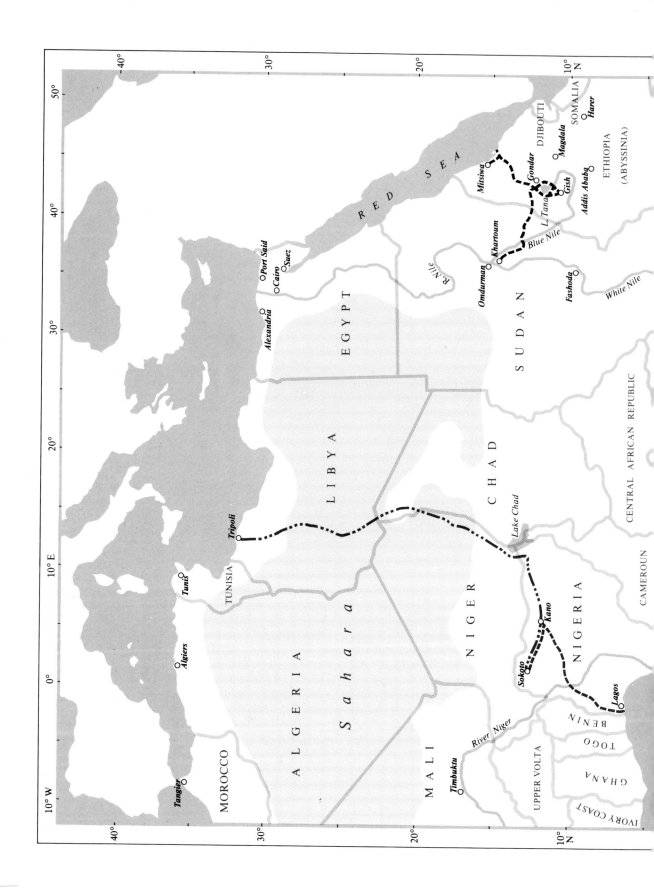

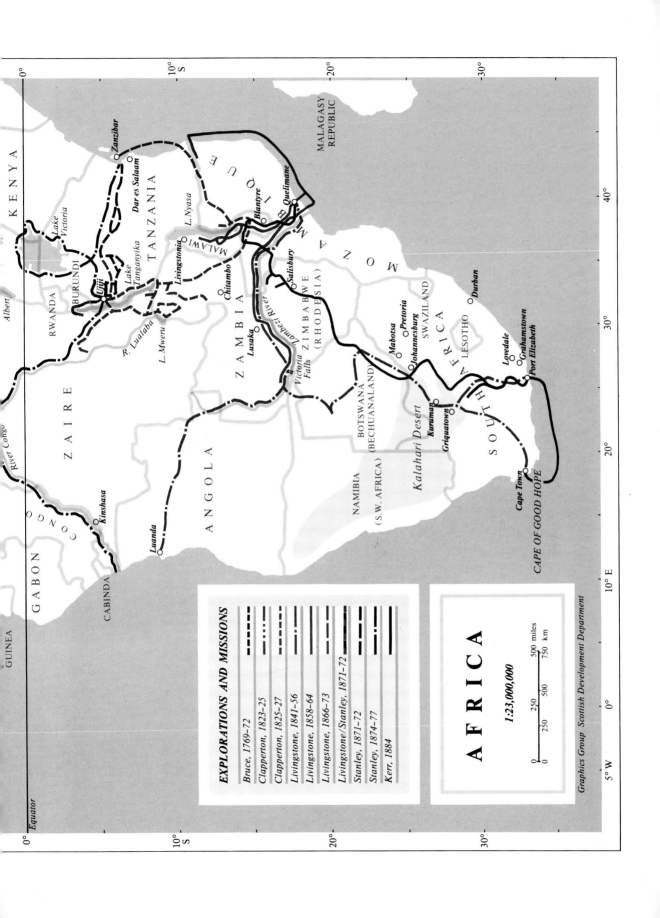

EXPLORATIONS AND MISSIONS

Bruce, 1769–72
Clapperton, 1823–25
Clapperton, 1825–27
Livingstone, 1841–56
Livingstone, 1858–64
Livingstone, 1866–73
Livingstone/Stanley, 1871–72
Stanley, 1871–72
Stanley, 1874–77
Kerr, 1884

A F R I C A

1:23,000,000

| 0 | 250 | 500 miles |
| 0 | 250 | 500 | 750 km |

Graphics Group Scottish Development Department

GUINEA

GABON

CONGO

ZAIRE

River Congo

Kinshasa

CABINDA

Luanda

ANGOLA

NAMIBIA
(S.W. AFRICA)

Kalahari Desert

BOTSWANA
(BECHUANALAND)

Cape Town
CAPE OF GOOD HOPE

KENYA

Lake
Victoria

RWANDA

BURUNDI

Albert

Ujiji

Lake
Tanganyika

R. Lualaba

L. Mweru

TANZANIA

Zanzibar

Dar es Salaam

Livingstonia

Chitambo

L. Nyasa

MALAWI

Blantyre

Quelimane

MOZAMBIQUE

MALAGASY
REPUBLIC

ZAMBIA

Lusaka

Zambezi River

Victoria
Falls

ZIMBABWE
(RHODESIA)

Salisbury

Mabotsa

Pretoria

Johannesburg

SWAZILAND

Durban

LESOTHO

SOUTH AFRICA

Kuruman

Griquatown

Lovedale
Grahamstown
Port Elizabeth

Equator

0°

10°
S

20°

30°

5° W   0°   10° E   20°   30°   40°

0°

10°
S

20°

30°

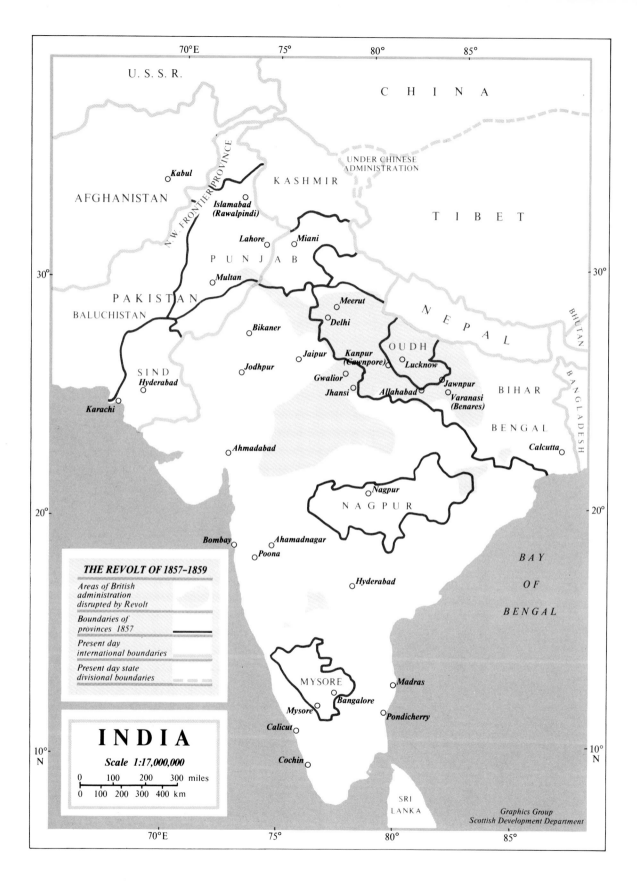

70°E   75°   80°   85°

U.S.S.R.

CHINA

KASHMIR

UNDER CHINESE
ADMINISTRATION

Kabul

AFGHANISTAN

N.W. FRONTIER PROVINCE

TIBET

Islamabad
(Rawalpindi)

Lahore   Miani

PUNJAB

30°

Multan

PAKISTAN

NEPAL

BALUCHISTAN

Bikaner

Meerut

Delhi

BHUTAN

BANGLADESH

Jaipur

Kanpur
(Cawnpore)

OUDH

Lucknow

SIND

Jodhpur

Hyderabad

Gwalior

Jhansi

Jawnpur

Allahabad

Varanasi
(Benares)

BIHAR

Karachi

BENGAL

Ahmadabad

Calcutta

Nagpur

20°

NAGPUR

20°

Bombay

Ahamadnagar

Poona

BAY

OF

THE REVOLT OF 1857–1859

*Areas of British
administration
disrupted by Revolt*

*Boundaries of
provinces 1857*

*Present day
international boundaries*

*Present day state
divisional boundaries*

Hyderabad

BENGAL

MYSORE

Madras

INDIA

Scale 1:17,000,000

Bangalore

Mysore

Pondicherry

0   100   200   300 miles

Calicut

0   100 200 300 400 km

Cochin

SRI
LANKA

10°
N

10°
N

Graphics Group
Scottish Development Department

70°E   75°   80°   85°

SCOTTISH EMPIRE
North America

CANADA: THE BEGINNING OF SCOTTISH COLONISATION

The seventeenth century marked the beginning of Scottish colonial enterprise. Scotland was still oriented towards Europe: discontented, ambitious or adventurous Scots had traditionally gravitated to Northern Europe as wandering scholars, craftsmen, traders or soldiers of fortune. By the mid-seventeenth century almost all the countries of Western Europe had planted settlements in the New World. Spain and Portugal laid claim to the whole of South and Central America. In North America England gained a foothold in Virginia and France at Port Royal and Quebec. Under James VI and I Scotland also entered the competition with the founding of New Scotland or Nova Scotia.

The colony was to provide a strategic barrier between the British territory of New England and the expanding French settlements along the St Lawrence River. Control of the St Lawrence became a vital issue in the bitter struggle for colonial supremacy which lasted until 1763 when Britain acquired the whole of North America. Extensive Scottish settlement resumed with the ending of the French domination, and from the late eighteenth century Scottish fur-traders joined in the opening up of North America through exploration.

Sir William Alexander, 1st Earl of Stirling
about 1567–1640

In 1621 James VI and I granted William Alexander of Menstrie a vast tract of land in North America extending from modern Nova Scotia and New Brunswick to Cape Breton Island and Prince Edward Island to form the colony of New Scotland. This was an extraordinary gesture in view of Alexander's credentials: his reputation rested on his sonnets, his Senecan tragedies and his classical knowledge which had persuaded the King to appoint him tutor to Prince Henry. His chief assets as a statesman were optimism and his association with the English colonisers of Newfoundland and New England.

Social and economic circumstances should have favoured Alexander's venture. Scottish emigration to Ulster was declining as the supply of land diminished, and the King actively discouraged Scottish migrations to the South and the Continent. The colonisation of Nova Scotia was deliberately designed as a means of 'disburdening this his Majesty's said ancient kingdom of all such younger brothers and mean gentlemen, who otherwise must be troublesome to the houses and friends from whence

9

Sir William Alexander, Earl of Stirling, poet, statesman and founder of Nova Scotia. Sir Thomas Urquhart of Cromarty said of him: 'He was born a poet and aimed to be a king.'

they are descended . . . or betake themselves to foreign work or baser shifts.' Alexander's pioneers sailed in 1622 and 1623, but failed to promote a permanent settlement. In 1625 he re-launched his project in *An Encouragement to Colonies*. As an additional attraction James VI founded the Order of the Knights Baronets of Nova Scotia, modelled on a similar scheme with which he had financed the Scottish plantation of Ulster. Heritable baronetcies were available to any gentleman willing to raise six settlers and contribute one thousand merks Scots (about £55 sterling) to the colonisation fund. Since the titles had to be conferred within the territory of New Scotland, a plot of ground within Edinburgh Castle was declared to be part of Nova Scotia for all time and the baronets were exempted from leaving Scotland. Despite the disappointing response the Order outlived its function and still exists today.

Alexander himself was probably unaware of the full political implications of his initiative. England had claimed the whole of North America on the strength of John Cabot's discoveries in 1491. Under Henri IV France set out to validate a rival claim based on Jacques Cartier's exploration of the St Lawrence. In 1627 French ambitions were reasserted with the formation of the Company of New France for the systematic colonisation of North America including Nova Scotia. When war broke out between England and France, a fleet of Scottish merchants seized Port Royal (Annapolis Royal) and Quebec. In 1629 a party of colonists landed on Cape Breton Island under the leadership of Alexander's son. On the conclusion of peace the personal interests of Charles I became implicated in the future of the Scottish colony when France refused to pay the dowry due upon his marriage to Henrietta Maria unless the disputed territory were ceded. Charles I agreed to the surrender of Nova Scotia and ordered the evacuation of the Scots.

For the rest of the century Scottish attention was diverted from North America. Alexander planned another settlement in Maine and other colonies were set up in East New Jersey and South Carolina and in the 1690s at Darien near Panama. The Darien colony was a secondary development which arose out of a commercial enterprise by 'The Company of Scotland trading to Africa and the Indies'. In an attempt to break the trade monopoly of the English-dominated East India Company, an international emporium was established on the Isthmus of Panama as the axis of Scottish trade with the Atlantic, the Pacific and the Americas. As a prospective New Caledonia Darien attracted over two thousand emigrants, of whom only a handful returned to Scotland when the surviving settlers were dispersed by Spanish forces. The fiasco of the Darien Scheme, which Scots attributed to William III's reluctance to support his Scottish subjects, finally discredited the idea of independent Scottish colonisation.

THE EMIGRATION BUSINESS

The 'epidemical fever of emigration' described by Dr Johnson began to affect Scotland seriously by the mid-eighteenth century. The main causes, rural poverty and over-population in relation to resources, were exacerbated by the improvement of farming techniques and were not eliminated by the expansion of trade following the Union of 1707. Most of the Scottish emigrants were drawn to America. Others joined the new Highland regiments raised for the Seven Years War and many of General Wolfe's Highlanders who had campaigned against the French settled in Canada after 1763. Large-scale emigration ceased temporarily during the American War of Independence. In the 1780s the process of depopulation accelerated in the Highlands owing to rising rents and the introduction of sheep farming as a more effective means of utilising land previously given over to subsistence farming and cattle raising. Arising from the changing pattern of Highland agriculture, the 'Clearances' or eviction of tenants from their ancestral holdings, became one of the most emotive issues in Scottish history. Attempts to re-settle crofters in coastal areas where they could supplement their livelihood by fishing and 'kelping' and offers of alternative employment in the new textile industries did not halt the mass exodus to the Lowlands and the colonies.

During the severe economic depression of the post-Napoleonic period government policy on emigration was gradually transformed. Official opposition had previously been based on the equation of population and wealth. A tentative gesture towards sponsored emigration was the settlement of discharged soldiers in Canada after Waterloo to alleviate unemployment in Britain and to counteract the threat of sedition caused by an influx of settlers from independent America. In general the Treasury still preferred to leave the initiative to speculative companies such as Galt's Canada Company which undertook to settle undeveloped land at their own expense and hoped to profit from the resale.

Under Queen Victoria the first permanent emigration department was created in 1837. 'Assisted emigration' came to be regarded as a panacea – a remedy for social discontent, a provider of markets and raw materials, and an expedient for fulfilling the expansionist and mercenary ambitions of Empire. Settlers like the Scots Canadian James B Brown complained, however, that the government financed 'the classes of persons who are over-abundant at home and consequently least wanted . . . Broken-spirited paupers, hand-loom weavers (from the west of Scotland) and other persons . . . unfit for the kinds of labour in demand by the colony . . . Irish labourers, who either cannot or will not work, except upon canals . . . and are the cause of serious disturbances . . .' The 'hungry Forties' saw the formation of charitable emigration societies which were later backed by trade unions. By the 1850s Scottish emigration to Canada was declining. Imperial wars and the new colonies of Australia and New Zealand presented other opportunities.

Archibald, 13th Laird of MacNab
1777–1860

The last Laird of MacNab, notorious coloniser of Upper Canada. 'For the last fifteen years we have been persecuted, harassed with lawsuits, threatened with deprivation of our lands and subjected to threats by the MacNab. The said Chief has impoverished many families and completely ruined others . . . Your petitioners have hitherto resisted, and will continue to resist, any attempt to impose the feudal system of the Dark Ages on them or their descendants.' (Petition from the settlers of MacNab township to the British Government 1839.)

One of the most eccentric and unscrupulous promoters of emigration in the nineteenth century was the 13th and last acknowledged Laird of MacNab. In 1822 he fled his ancestral home in Killin, Perthshire, to escape his creditors and made his way to Canada with the aim of raising money to redeem his estates. His apparent importance persuaded the Canadian authorities to allocate him a township of 81,000 acres on the Ottawa river. Emigration from the Highlands tended to be a communal undertaking reflecting the close-knit structure of local society. The progressive decline of the family fortunes had caused a large number of MacNabs to settle in Canada at the turn of the century and their chief intended to exploit traditional clan loyalties to achieve a wholesale transplantation to the township named after him.

Following a succession of poor harvests in Perthshire, the first crofters left in 1825. Officially the MacNab was an agent of the government which offered a free grant of land to all able-bodied emigrants. To his colonists he presented himself as the sole proprietor of the township and demanded payment in kind in lieu of rent. By the 1830s the settlers had grown restive under his feudal tyranny. An official enquiry into their complaints led to the confiscation of all his land and the restitution of all his illegal exactions to the settlers. After his eviction the colony, based on Arnprior, flourished as a farming and lumbering centre. MacNab never conceded that any deception had been practised and in 1848 left Canada for good, convinced that he was 'the most wronged man in Canada, a leader of men, betrayed by his own serfs.' As his Scottish estates had been sold to his chief creditor, he retired to Orkney where his mistress bore him a child in his eightieth year. The ensuing scandal forced him to retreat to France where he died.

MacNab's estimate of his own status underlies the only known portrait of him, a primitive likeness which was probably painted in Canada. It may well have been inspired by Raeburn's powerful portrait of the 12th Laird as Lieutenant of the Breadalbane Volunteers which could have been familiar to the Canadian artist through an engraving. Alternatively, MacNab may have described the portrait of his flamboyant uncle in the hope of being immortalised through a similarly grandiose and romantic presentation of leadership in Highland society.

The 12th Laird of MacNab by Sir Henry Raeburn. Sir Thomas Lawrence is said to have declared it the best portrait he had ever seen.

John Galt
1779–1839

John Galt in later life by Charles Grey.

'But when my numerous books are forgotten, I shall yet be remembered . . . I contrived the Canada Company, which will hereafter be spoken of among the eras of a nation destined to greatness.'

Galt's confident self-assessment in his *Literary Life* (1834) has ironically been reversed by posterity: the controversial founder of the Canada Company is now remembered as the author of *The Annals of the Parish* and other sketches of Scottish rural life which look forward to the 'kailyard' novels of the mid- to late nineteenth century. In the early nineteenth century he was probably the greatest single contributor to the colonisation of Canada. His involvement in Canadian affairs began with his appointment in 1820 as London agent for the claims of Canadian victims of the Anglo-American war of 1812–14. In 1826 he founded the Canada Company to develop a large area of un-exploited Crown land in Upper Canada (modern Ontario). At this time North America was divided into the two British protectorates of Upper and Lower Canada. Lower Canada was dominated by French settlement; development in the upper province was minimal. Although the Company's agents were active in England and Ireland as well as Edinburgh and Glasgow, it appealed primarily to Scots. Under Galt's administration colonies were established in Guelph and Goderich. Galt the philanthropist did not support the policy of 'shovelling out paupers' and stressed the need to attract capital investment by recruiting resourceful, educated and fairly prosperous pioneers. There were to be no free grants of land and colonies must become self-supporting. A further proposal to lure younger sons of the landed gentry through a scheme comparable to that of the Nova Scotia baronetcies was not ratified by government.

In 1829, during a crisis in the Canada Company, Galt fell foul of officialdom and was recalled to Britain. As soon as his disgrace became common knowledge his creditors closed in and he was imprisoned for debt. In order to ease his situation he reverted to his second career of literature. *Lawrie Todd*, a novel based on the real life experience of a Scottish emigrant to America, appeared the following year. In 1834, when the Canada Company's shares had recovered, Galt decided to form the British American Land Company to operate in Lower Canada with special reference to Highland emigrants. His own prospects failed to improve and five years later he died in poverty in Greenock. His youngest son Alexander, a director of the new Company, made his fortune in Canada on the South Alberta coalfields, founded Lethbridge, and rose to high office as Finance Minister and a 'Father of Confederation'. The Canada Company flourished, surviving until 1953.

The Founding of Guelph in 1827

Galt's difficulties with the management of the Canada Company were partly occasioned by a difference of priorities. Whereas the Directors demanded a prompt return for their capital, Galt continued to envisage his colonies as 'an asylum for the exiles of

13

John Galt sketched by Daniel Maclise for *Fraser's Magazine for Town and Country* in 1830. 'But when my numerous books are forgotten . . . I shall yet be remembered . . . I contrived the Canada Company, which will hereafter be spoken of among the eras of a nation destined to greatness.'

so-called society – a refuge for the fleers from the old world and its systems fore-doomed.' Something of this attitude is captured in his mock-heroic account of the founding of Guelph, self-deprecating and yet filled with the sense of a momentous occasion, of 'making history'. The appointed day was 23 April, St George's day, and the name of Guelph was chosen as a compliment to George IV.

'Next morning we walked after breakfast towards the site which had been selected . . . about eighteen miles from Galt . . . Scarcely . . . had we entered the bush, as the woods are called, when the doctor found he had lost the way . . . After wandering up and down like the two babes, with not even the comfort of a blackberry . . . we discovered a hut . . . inhabited by a Dutch shoemaker . . . With his assistance we reached the skirts of the wild to which we were going, and were informed in the cabin of a squatter that all our men had gone forward. About sunset, dripping wet, we arrived near the spot we were in quest of, a shanty, which an Indian, who had committed murder, had raised as a refuge for himself . . . Dr Dunlop, having doffed his wet garb, and dressed himself Indian fashion in blankets, we proceeded with Mr Prior, attended by two woodmen with their axes.

It was consistent with my plan to invest our ceremony with a little mystery, the better to make it remembered . . . So, intimating that the main body of the men were not to come, we walked to the brow of the neighbouring rising ground . . . and . . . a large maple tree was chosen; on which, taking an axe from one of the woodmen, I struck the first stroke. To me at least the moment was impressive, – and the silence of the woods, that echoed to the sound, was as the sign of the solemn genius of the wilderness departing for ever . . . The tree fell with a crash of accumulating thunder, as if ancient Nature were alarmed at the entrance of social man into her innocent solitudes with his sorrows, his follies and his crimes . . . The doctor pulled a flask of whisky from his bosom, and we drank prosperity to the City of Guelph.'

(*Autobiography* 1833)

When Galt returned to Britain after his much publicised 'dismissal' from the Company he sat to Daniel Maclise for a portrait which vindicated his own image of himself. The drawing was immediately adapted for reproduction in a character sketch in *Fraser's Magazine for Town and Country* to which Galt was a regular contributor. His biographer, noting his 'liberality in the article of trowsers . . . ready manufactured by the axe or saw of a Canadian backwoodsman', commented: 'We see that Galt turns his back also upon Canada, which we hope is by no means typical of an intention never to turn again towards the colony he has created, and the towns he has raised.'

Lochaber No More by John Watson Nicol: 'the tragedy of the Highland shepherd's life' viewed from the 1880s.

Canadian Boat Song

Listen to me, as when ye heard our father
Sing long ago the songs of other shores;
Listen to me, and then in chorus gather
All your deep voices, as ye pull your oars;
Fair these broad meads, these hoary woods are grand;
But we are exiles from our father's land.

From the lone shieling of the misty island
Mountains divide us, and the waste of seas –
Yet still the blood is strong, the heart is Highland,
And we in dreams behold the Hebrides.
Fair these broad meads . . .

We ne'er shall tread the fancy-haunted valley,
Where 'tween the dark hills creeps the small clear stream,
In arms around the patriarch banner rally,
Nor see the moon on royal tombstones gleam;
Fair these broad meads . . .

15

When the bold kindred, in the time long vanish'd
Conquer'd the soil and fortified the keep, –
No seer foretold the children would be banish'd,
That a degenerate Lord might boast his sheep:
Fair these broad meads . . .

Come foreign rage – let Discord burst in slaughter!
O then for clansmen true, and stern claymore –
The hearts that would have given their blood like water,
Beat heavily beyond the Atlantic roar:
Fair these broad meads . . .

These anonymous verses were first published as a 'translation from the Gaelic' in *Blackwood's Magazine*, September 1829, and were much quoted throughout the nineteenth century, being variously attributed to many leading authors including John Galt and James Hogg, the Ettrick Shepherd. John Watson Nicol's painting *Lochaber No More* (1883) suggests a similar attitude towards Highland emigration and the particular view of the Clearances which had become embedded in folk memory.

THE SEARCH FOR A NORTH-WEST PASSAGE

The quest for a North-West Passage linking the Atlantic and Pacific Oceans was the indirect result of the voyages of Columbus who had sought a short route to the fabulous wealth of the Indies by sailing west from Spain. In 1492 he discovered the unknown continent of America which he imagined to be the east coast of Asia. The gradual realisation of Columbus's error led to an intensive search for a way either by north or by south through the newly discovered land barrier stretching from the Arctic to the Antarctic. Initially a south-eastern route was explored, the first European navigator to reach India by sea being the Portuguese Vasco da Gama who succeeded in rounding the Cape of Good Hope in 1497. An alternative route was found in 1520 when Magellan negotiated the Straits between the South American continent and Tierra del Fuego and completed the first circumnavigation of the world. Spain and Portugal now controlled the two known commercial sea routes to the Orient and planned to divide any new colonies between them.

Under Henry VII England built up a merchant navy capable of challenging the maritime supremacy and trade monopoly of Spain and Portugal. English efforts were concentrated on the attempt to shorten the voyage to the Indies. The idea of a passage to the north of the American continent was conceived by John Cabot, a Venetian trader settled in London. For the next three centuries the discovery of a North-West or a North-East Passage became the principal lure to Arctic navigators.

From the mid-eighteenth century the project was temporarily abandoned. An isolated attempt by Captain Cook in 1776 ended in his death on the Hawaiian Islands. At the turn of the century the navy was fully occupied with wars and it was only after the fall of Napoleon that the search could be resumed, giving rise to the greatest period of Arctic exploration in British history. By now the motivation had changed from the commercial to the scientific: it was obvious that a northern passage could have no economic importance, being frozen for most of the year. Official participation began in 1818 with Sir John Ross and continued almost annually until 1845 when Sir John Franklin's expedition vanished in the Arctic. The eventual discovery of a North-West Passage by Robert McClure was the incidental outcome of the long and harrowing search for Franklin. The Passage was finally negotiated from end to end in 1903 by the Norwegian explorer Roald Amundsen.

Major Voyages in Search of a North-West Passage

John Cabot	1497, 1498
Sebastian Cabot	1508–1509
Jacques Cartier	1534, 1535–1536, 1541
Martin Frobisher	1576, 1577, 1578
John Davis	1585, 1586, 1587
Henry Hudson	1609, 1610–1611
William Baffin	1615, 1616
James Cook	1776
John Ross	1818
William Edward Parry	1819, 1821, 1824
John Ross	1829–1833
Sir John Franklin	1845 . . .

Reverend William Scoresby
1789–1857

By the late sixteenth century England was actively engaged in the international whale fisheries off Greenland and Newfoundland, one of the chief promoters of English interests being the powerful group of Merchant Adventurers who constituted the Muscovy Company. After suffering a decline in the following century the industry was revitalised with government support in the mid-eighteenth century, operating mainly from London, Hull and Whitby. This revival extended to Scotland and in the 1750s Edinburgh ladies were able to order hoops and stays made from whalebone brought home by Scottish ships.

Of necessity whalers were also scientists and geographers who played a vital if unofficial role in Arctic exploration. William Scoresby was typical and yet exceptional in building up a scientific reputation far beyond the demands of his calling. He began his annual voyages to Greenland at the age of ten as an apprentice to his father, a Whitby whaler. In 1806 the Scoresbys reached latitude 81° 30′ north, the furthest point ever recorded by a sailing vessel. On his return the younger Scoresby enrolled at Edinburgh University and was introduced to Sir Joseph Banks, the President of the Royal Society of London, to whom he regularly reported his Arctic discoveries. In 1817 he described an unprecedented break up of the polar ice barrier from the eastern coast of Greenland to Spitzbergen which for centuries had prevented any extensive penetration into the Arctic Ocean.

Reverend William Scoresby, whaler, Arctic scientist and clergyman, photographed by D O Hill and Robert Adamson in 1844.

He urged Banks to seize the opportunity to launch a scientific expedition in search of a North-West Passage. Scoresby's revelation provided a decisive impetus to nineteenth-century exploration which culminated in the discovery of a Passage and the location of the North Magnetic Pole. The command of the first official expedition, however, was given to Captain John Ross, a naval officer without Arctic experience.

Public interest stimulated by Ross's expedition created a demand for authentic information on the polar regions. In 1819, following his election to the Royal Society of Edinburgh, Scoresby published a pioneering *Account of the Arctic Regions*. On his annual voyage in 1821–2 he carried out the first detailed survey of the east coast of Greenland, commemorated by the naming of Scoresby Land and Scoresby Sound. The next year he abandoned whaling to enter the ministry. Scoresby continued his research in oceanography, meteorology and magnetism with undiminished energy while at the same time initiating a campaign for industrial and educational reform in his parish of Bradford. In 1831 he had been elected a founder-member of the British Association for the Advancement of Science. He remained a regular contributor and it was at the 1844 meeting of the Association in York that he was photographed by the Edinburgh calotypists D O Hill and Robert Adamson.

Admiral Sir John Ross
1777–1856

Admiral Sir John Ross in the year of his second polar expedition of 1829.

'I am persuaded that a north-west passage exists – that is, as regards any obstruction from land; but how far it may or may not be blocked up with ice, so as to be always impervious, can only be determined by repeated trials.'

(William Scoresby to Sir Joseph Banks 1818)

In 1818 the Admiralty appointed Captain John Ross of Wigtownshire to command the first of a series of government-sponsored expeditions in search of a North-West Passage. Following the defeat of Napoleon Britain was eager to demonstrate her continuing maritime supremacy. By adopting Scoresby's proposal, the government was upholding the national honour and complying with the Royal Society's injunction to explore the Arctic as an untapped source of scientific knowledge. The results were not impressive: Ross charted the coast of Davis Strait, discovered a new tribe of Eskimos and helped to extend the whaling grounds to Baffin Island, but denied the existence of a Passage. On entering Lancaster Sound (which later proved to be the eastern end of a Passage) he had been deluded into thinking that it was enclosed by mountains. A bitter controversy developed when Ross's lieutenant Parry questioned the accuracy of his observations. Ross was discredited in official and public estimation and the next expedition was entrusted to Parry.

In the hope of vindicating himself Ross again approached the Admiralty in 1828 with an innovatory project for an expedition based on steam navigation (previous Arctic expeditions had relied on converted whalers). Eventually he secured the backing of Sir Felix Booth, the manufacturer of Booth's Gin. Ross's second expedition of 1829–33 set a record of survival in the Arctic over four winters. With his nephew James Clark Ross he discovered and named after his patron the Gulf and Isthmus of 'Boothia Felix', surveyed King William Island and a vast stretch of coastline and located the North Magnetic Pole. He returned to a hero's welcome and a knighthood. His last Arctic voyage was undertaken in 1850 as part of the massive search for Sir John Franklin. Overshadowed by the reputation of Parry and Franklin, Ross's greatest contribution lay in the training of a whole generation of polar explorers.

A Polar Entertainment

The publicity which greeted Ross when he returned from his second polar expedition in 1833 was quite sensational. The spectacle advertised at Robert Burford's panorama theatre in Leicester Square was some measure of the appeal which Arctic exploration now held for the British public. As popular excitement mounted scenes of polar desolation were added to the standard panorama repertoire of natural phenomena, battles, naval engagements and foreign scenery: in 1822 a panorama of the North Pole was exhibited by the proprietor of the Egyptian Hall in London and in 1830 David Roberts devised a moving diorama of Parry's expedition in search of a North-West Passage. By the turn of the nineteenth century the panorama (which, in its more elaborate versions such as the diorama invented by Daguerre, was the cultural and social forerunner of cinema) had become an immensely popular form of entertainment with a public who had little chance of travelling abroad in the days before the introduction of Cook's tours.

Descriptive pamphlet issued to visitors to Robert Burford's popular panorama of the Arctic regions charted by Ross.

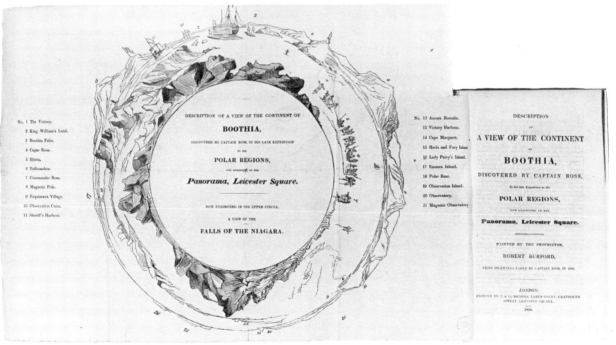

19

The principle of the panorama as an optical entertainment was conceived by Robert Barker, an Irish portrait painter working in Edinburgh, when he noticed the brilliant effect of light falling vertically on the wall of his darkened debtor's cell. In 1787 he patented his idea and took to painting vast continuous views of capital cities, beginning with one of Edinburgh which was shown there the following year. The pictures, executed in a broad style akin to theatrical scene painting, were usually stretched round the walls of a large cylinder and lit from above so that the spectators, placed in semi-darkness at a central vantage point, were treated to an astonishing illusion of reality and gradually lost all judgement of distance and space in the external world. In 1789 Barker moved to London where he operated from a specifically designed, double-decker 'rotunda' in Leicester Square. After his death the business was developed by his son Henry Aston Barker in association with Robert Burford and did not close down until 1865. Increasingly sophisticated techniques were evolved in the 1820s, 1830s, and 1840s with the addition of ingenious sound and lighting effects and the incorporation of three-dimensional objects to heighten the illusion of reality. Artists vied with each other to produce the most spectacular painting of all time and the largest, a view of London shown in 1829, covered over an acre of canvas.

John Sakeouse
1797–1819

Sir John Ross's Eskimo interpreter, John Sakeouse – a contemporary engraving reflecting the sensation caused by his arrival in Leith.

For centuries it was common practice among European explorers to abduct living natives as hostages or ethnographic curiosities for public display. As early as the sixteenth century Eskimos are known to have been captured by Martin Frobisher and John Davis. Although Sakeouse was probably not the first Eskimo to reach Scotland – alleged sightings off the coast of Scotland were reported in the seventeenth and eighteenth centuries – he was almost certainly the first to come voluntarily.

At the close of the fishing season in 1816 Sakeouse stowed away on a Greenland whaler, the *Thomas and Ann* of Leith. Having been converted to Christianity by missionaries, he intended to visit their country and return home as a missionary himself when he had studied the Scriptures and the art of drawing for which he had a particular inclination. The sensation which he caused is minutely recorded in the inscription attached to an engraved portrait after Amelia Anderson, a delightful example of contemporary fascination with the weird and wonderful aspects of 'primitive', non-Western cultures, combined with more or less complacent ignorance.

'In the month of August, 1816, he arrived at Leith, in the Thomas & Ann, Greenland Whaler, and exhibited several feats of dexterity with his lance and Canoe, which attracted great attention, and gave rise to another exhibition of his powers, in the presence of the greatest concourse of spectators ever known to have assembled at Leith. He successfully contended in swiftness with a six oared Whale Boat and in his

A study of John Sakeouse by the landscape painter, Alexander Nasmyth. According to *Blackwood's Magazine*, 'About the beginning of 1818, Mr Nasmyth, the eminent artist of this city, accidentally met John Sakeouse in the streets of Leith, and having some years before been engaged to execute a set of drawings of the Esquimaux costume, he was naturally attracted by his appearance, although his dress was a good deal modified by his European habits. Mr Nasmyth brought him up to Edinburgh, and finding that he had not only a taste for drawing, but considerable readiness of execution, very kindly offered to give him instructions.'

course, threw his Lance with unerring certainty against the bulb of the Beacon. The Canoe weighs 16lbs: the Vignette shews its size and shape, and how he fixes himself in it; thus fixed, he manages it with such agility as in an instant to dive, turning the keel of the Canoe directly upwards; and then in a moment replace himself. He has made considerable progress already in speaking, reading and writing of the English language. He says he was at School in his own country; had read of England; and he is even acquainted with several Historical Facts. When shown a representation of an Elephant, he was much delighted, and said he had heard of the animal but had never seen a likeness of it before. His mother tongue strikingly resembles that of the natives in the interior of Africa.'

In 1817 Sakeouse decided to settle in Britain on learning of the death of his only surviving relative. While living in Leith he was noticed by the celebrated Scottish landscape painter Alexander Nasmyth who had recently been commissioned to produce studies of Eskimo costume. Nasmyth gave him some instruction in drawing and introduced him to Sir James Hall, the President of the Royal Society of Edinburgh, in the hope that Hall's intervention might secure him a place on Captain John Ross's forthcoming expedition to the Arctic. The recommendation having been accepted, Sakeouse was engaged as official interpreter and took the chance to try out his newly acquired skill, as may be seen from the watercolour reproduced in Ross's account of his first polar voyage – 'the first specimen we had witnessed of his talents for historical composition.' The scene shows the meeting of Captain Ross (the shorter figure) and Lieutenant Parry with the Etah Eskimos whom Ross named 'the Arctic Highlanders'. His two converted whalers the *Isabella* and the *Alexander* are moored to the ice. In the background Sakeouse has depicted himself in a beaver hat exchanging presents of shirts, mirrors and beads for narwhals' horns, knives and sea-horse teeth.

On his return from the Arctic Sakeouse was fêted in London and then sent to Edinburgh to continue his formal education. He also resumed drawing lessons and was warmly encouraged by the Nasmyth family in his efforts to master English. Unfortunately he succumbed to typhoid before he could take part in any further expeditions. Such was his popularity that a long obituary appeared in *Blackwood's Magazine* for 1818–19 with an edifying description of his death-bed piety.

THE FRANKLIN TRAGEDY

In 1845 the Admiralty sent out its last and most elaborate expedition in response to mounting pressure from the British public. Command of the expedition was first offered to Sir John Ross's distinguished nephew, the Antarctic explorer James Clark Ross, who refused it on the grounds of age. The second

21

FIRST COMMUNICATION with the NATIVES of PRINCE REGENTS BAY, as Drawn by JOHN SACKHEOUSE and Presented to CAP.T ROSS. Aug.t 10.1818.

London Published Oct.r 1819 by John Murray, Albemarle Street

A watercolour by John Sakeouse illustrating the encounter between Sir John Ross and the 'Arctic Highlanders' – 'the first specimen we had witnessed of his talents for historical composition.'

Sir John Franklin, the tragic hero of nineteenth-century polar exploration, who vanished without trace in the Arctic in 1845.

candidate was Sir John Franklin who at the age of fifty-nine was the doyen of British Arctic explorers.

Franklin's ships *Erebus* and *Terror* were last sighted by whalers in 1845 in the north of Baffin Bay. After two years of silence popular demand and vigorous campaigning by Sir John Ross, a close friend of Franklin, forced the government to embark on a ten-year search for the lost explorer. The first definitive news was brought by Dr John Rae. Only later did it become apparent that Franklin's team had effectively discovered a Passage – at the cost of an entire expedition. In the meantime the greater part of the Canadian archipelago had been surveyed and mapped in the course of the manhunt.

The cult of Franklin as a tragic hero surpassed even that of Livingstone. In the words of Roald Amundsen who navigated Franklin's Passage in 1903: 'No tragedy of the Polar ice has so stirred mankind as that of Franklin and his crew, stirred them not simply to sorrow but also to stubborn resumption of the struggle.'

Dr John Rae
1813–1893

The pioneers of the Canadian fur trade were French settlers who gathered beaver pelts from the Indians of the St Lawrence valley. In the reign of Charles II the English seized the initiative by setting up the London-based Hudson's Bay Company in 1670. The Company was rapidly taken over by 'douce Scots gentlemen' with a staff of Orkneymen recruited when ships touched at the Orkneys before crossing the Atlantic. Scottish enterprise helped to build an impressive record of exploration in North America by Company traders.

The outstanding Scot in Company service, John Rae, was an Orkney surgeon who followed in the tradition of the fur-trader turned explorer with an exceptional capacity for physical endurance. In the impression of a contemporary: 'He was very muscular and active, full of animal spirits, and had a fine intellectual countenance. He was considered . . . to be one of the best snow-shoe walkers in the service, was also an excellent rifle-shot, and could stand an immense amount of fatigue.' By common consent Rae was the most successful overland Arctic explorer of the mid-nineteenth century. His methods of living off the land by hunting and fishing in native style ran counter to those of the costly British naval expeditions and enabled him to achieve unprecedented records of travel. On his first major expedition of 1846–7 Rae was delegated by the Company to complete the survey of the Arctic coastline of North America begun by Ross and Parry and also by other Company personnel. By the end of the expedition Rae Strait had been discovered and the entire coastline mapped with the exception of Boothia Peninsula. Soon afterwards Rae was drawn into the search for Sir John Franklin – the motive of his most rewarding expedition. Within a single season in 1851 he covered over one thousand miles by sledge from the Great Bear Lake to Wollaston Peninsula and Victoria Island and then up the Coppermine River, totalling some five thousand three hundred miles in eight months.

In 1853 Rae set out on his last expedition for the Company. The following spring at Pelly Bay he encountered Eskimos from whom he obtained the first news of Franklin. He inferred that Franklin's crew must have died of starvation near the estuary of the Great Fish River. Relics purchased from the Eskimos (and later deposited in the National Maritime Museum and the Royal Scottish Museum) established beyond doubt the identity of the missing white men. In the autumn of 1854 Rae sailed for Britain to collect the reward offered to the discoverer of Franklin's fate. The dramatic report which he submitted to the Admiralty was immediately printed in *The Times* and became the focus of a scandal provoked by his conclusions: 'From the mutilated state of many of the corpses and the contents of the kettles, it is evident that our wretched countrymen had been driven to the last resource – cannibalism – as a means of prolonging existence.' Lady Franklin, who bitterly contested the award of the prize-money to Rae, insisted that the mystery surrounding her husband's disappearance was still not entirely solved. An interlude followed during the Crimean War: naval resources

The Orkney surgeon Dr John Rae, an outstanding overland explorer in the service of the Hudson's Bay Company, recovered the first relics of the Franklin expedition.

were fully deployed and could not be diverted to the search for Franklin. In 1859 Lady Franklin financed a last expedition under McClintock with instructions to recover any survivors and to substantiate her claim that Franklin had succeeded in tracing a North-West Passage. Far from discrediting Rae, McClintock's definitive account of the tragedy confirmed both Lady Franklin's claim and Rae's most distressing allegations.

Vice-Admiral Sir Robert McClure
1807–1873

Sir Robert McClure discovered a North-West Passage in 1850 – in the words of Martin Frobisher, 'the only great thing left undone in the world'.

By the 1850s the British government was reluctant to continue the quest for a hypothetical and at best intractable North-West Passage. In 1850 the Admiralty capitulated in the face of public opinion and sponsored a further relief expedition in search of Sir John Franklin. The expedition was led by Captain Richard Collinson and Robert McClure of the *Investigator* who had recently served under Sir James Clark Ross on a similar mission.

After wintering in pack ice near Melville Sound, McClure forced his way overland to test the popular theory of a possible connection between Melville Sound and Barrow Strait – the missing link in the problem of the Passage. In October the Passage was sighted, over thirty years after the launching of the first British polar expedition under Sir John Ross. In the New Year McClure sent out search parties for Franklin. Over the following winter his ship was beset by ice and in 1852 the Admiralty despatched an expedition in search of both Franklin and McClure. McClure's party was finally rescued in 1853 and he was rewarded with a knighthood.

Although McClure was the first to trace a Passage from one ocean to the other, he did not confirm the existence of a navigable channel. When relics of the Franklin expedition were eventually recovered, it became clear that Franklin's men had forestalled McClure by locating an alternative route.

McClure's achievement was commemorated in a portrait by Stephen Pearce (now in the National Portrait Gallery in London) which shows the explorer dressed in the costume he wore in 1850 and which was one of a gallery of portraits commissioned by Sir John Barrow of the Admiralty, the chief official promoter of British Arctic exploration.

POSTSCRIPT

'And now there came both mist and snow,
And it grew wondrous cold:
And ice, mast high, came floating by
As green as emerald.'

Within a few years of the publication of Coleridge's *Ancient Mariner* at the turn of the nineteenth century Arctic exploration began to generate an excitement equal to that aroused by Cook's Pacific voyages. The renewed quest for a North-West Passage reached its climax with the ill-fated expedition of Sir John Franklin in 1845 and the fascination of the Arctic intensified when he became the object of the longest and most expensive manhunt of the century.

Millais' painting of 1874, *The North-West Passage*, is both a retrospective view and a piece of topical propaganda. Captain Trelawney, the model for the old sailor, belonged to the generation of Byron and Shelley, but he sat to Millais shortly before the proclamation of Queen Victoria as Empress of India. Seen in a context of British imperialism spreading its beneficent influence round the globe, the picture becomes a symbol of national pride: a Union Jack stands furled in one corner and a portrait of Nelson, the ultimate in British heroism and naval power, hangs above the sailor's head. The subtitle of the painting read: 'It might be done, and England should do it.' As early as 1818 a reviewer wrote at the time of Sir John Ross's first Arctic voyage: 'It would be somewhat mortifying if a naval power but of yesterday should complete a discovery in the nineteenth century which was so happily commenced by Englishmen in the sixteenth; and another Vespucius run away with the honours due to a Columbus.'

The North-West Passage by Sir John Everett Millais, 1874: 'It might be done and England should do it.'

The Arab Princess . . . 'Whose picture John Henderson caused take with her black maid after their own country habit.'

Africa

SIR JOHN HENDERSON 5th of FORDELL and THE ARAB PRINCESS: THE ARAB EMPIRE IN NORTH AFRICA

In the sixteenth and seventeenth centuries one of the most challenging careers open to the wandering Scot was that of a soldier of fortune in the armies of Europe. Scots swelled the forces of Denmark and Sweden during the Thirty Years War and formed the redoubtable Scots Brigade in the Netherlands. Sir John Henderson (died 1655), three of whose uncles served with the Scots Brigade, held a command in the Mediterranean where he probably campaigned for one of the southern European states against the Moors. In this way he accidentally became one of the first Scots to visit Africa – as a slave of the Arabs in Zanzibar. His adventures are recorded in the inscription on the portrait of the Arab princess commissioned by Sir John in memory of his rescuer: 'John Henderson of Fordel, traveling in his youth through several pairts of Asia and Africa from the year 1619 to the year 1628 was delivered into slavery by a Barbarian in Zanquebar [Zanzibar] on the coast of Africa where a Princess of that countrie falling in love with him even to renouncing her religion and country contrived the means of both their escape and getting aboard a ship trading up the red sea landed at Alexandria where she died, whose picture John Henderson caused take with her black maid after their own country habit [costume]. From the original picture at Oterston [Otterston near Aberdour in Fife] by W Frier 1731.' When he returned to Britain Sir John joined the royalist forces in the Civil War, receiving a commission together with Montrose 'to do mischief in Scotland.'

Apart from its romantic associations, the portrait of the Princess provides incidental evidence of Arab power in seventeenth-century Africa. The Arab invasion of North Africa began soon after the death in 632 of the Prophet Mohamet who had launched Islam as one of the world's leading religions. To the devout Muslim the 'jihad' or holy war against unbelievers was an obligation as binding as the creed of the one true God Allah. From Egypt the invaders swept on to conquer the 'Barbary' coast (modern Algeria, Tunisia and Morocco) and Spain. The only state to escape subjugation was the ancient Christian kingdom of Abyssinia, or Ethiopia, ruled by the legendary emperor Prester John.

The emergence of this vast Islamic empire effectively closed

Sir John Henderson of Fordell by George Jamesone.

the whole of North Africa to European penetration. The fifteenth-century Portuguese navigators who led the way in European exploration of Africa concentrated their attention on the coastal regions south of Arab territory. Later European explorers such as James Bruce 'the Abyssinian' had to depend on histories compiled by mediaeval Arab geographers for a working knowledge of the area. From the north the Arabs gradually advanced down the east coast as far as the river Zambesi, lured by the prospect of copper, slaves and ivory. In the early nineteenth century they finally seized control of the slave trade based on Zanzibar, which Livingstone spent his life trying to suppress.

EUROPE DISCOVERS AFRICA

In Africa the contribution of Scottish explorers was outstanding. Beginning with James Bruce in Abyssinia and Mungo Park in West Africa, it reached a peak in the 1860s with the discovery of the Nile source by Grant and his English companion Speke and the opening up of East Africa by Livingstone, the missionary-turned-explorer whose fame brought Stanley the journalistic scoop of the century.

The classic age of European exploration in Africa opened in 1769 with the travels of Bruce and drew to a close on the death of Livingstone a century later. The opening up of the 'Dark Continent' was a late development, delayed by Arab domination of the north, the natural obstacles of its geography, and the inhospitability of its climate which earned it a reputation as 'the white man's grave'. In spite of the pioneering voyages of the Portuguese in the fifteenth century, European knowledge of the interior remained almost nil for three hundred years. The situation was humorously summed up by Dean Swift:

' . . . Geographers in Afric-Maps
With Savage-Pictures fill their Gaps,
And o'er inhabitable Downs
Place Elephants for want of Towns.'

In the 1770s a population explosion and the first great burst of industrial expansion in Britain created a powerful stimulus to new activity overseas. The attractions of Africa as a second 'New World' were enhanced by the loss of Britain's transatlantic colonies through the American War of Independence. In 1788 Sir Joseph Banks founded the African Association, a gentleman's scientific and dining club which sponsored enlightened travellers or 'geographical missionaries' and became an influential pressure-group responsible for convincing government of the value of African exploration. Efforts were directed towards the four main river systems – the Niger, the Nile, the Zambesi and the Congo. The first objective was access to the interior of West Africa to exploit contacts already established through the slave trade. In the 1850s the centre of interest was transferred to the East by Livingstone. In this pre-colonial phase European expeditions were largely non-political, inspired by scientific curiosity, commercial enterprise and missionary zeal. The turning point came with Stanley's journeys in the Congo on behalf of King Leopold of the Belgians: from the 1870s exploration became a prelude to the 'Scramble for Africa'.

James Bruce of Kinnaird
1730–1794

In 1763 the Scottish landowner James Bruce was drawn to Africa by the offer of a consulate in Algiers and a commission from George III to record the splendid Roman remains in Algiers and Tunis for the royal collection. Landed gentry normally confined themselves to travels in Europe and the study of Greek and Roman antiquities in the Mediterranean countries. Bruce's remarkable decision to venture into Abyssinia at his own expense was predictably classical in inspiration. The mystery of the sources of the Nile had absorbed geographers since Roman times and would continue to defy solution until 1862. Abyssinia itself was an equal mystery, isolated from Europe for almost two centuries.

For all his pretensions to 'the taste and science of a scholar', Bruce embarked on his African adventure as though it were an extension of the Grand Tour of Europe which was considered vital to the education of any cultured Scottish gentleman. He prepared for his trip by studying in Rome with the eminent Scottish antiquary Andrew Lumisden and took the opportunity to have himself portrayed as the elegant grandee by Pompeo Batoni, the most fashionable painter of aristocratic travellers and social climbers in Italy. A miniature version of the picture was sent to his fiancée back in Scotland.

Unlike most Europeans Bruce adopted Arab dress once he reached Africa, travelling as a doctor under the name of El Hakim Yagoube. In this guise he gained the trust of the Abyssinian court, was created lord of Gish and campaigned for the emperor against his rebellious warlords. After many setbacks he confidently proclaimed his discovery of the source of the Nile in 1770. In reality he had revisited the springs of the Blue Nile described by Portuguese missionaries a hundred and fifty years earlier. The origin of the main branch, the White Nile, was still unknown.

Back in Britain Bruce's claims met with disbelief and even ridicule. John Kay's satirical etching shows him in conversation with Peter Williamson, compiler of the first Edinburgh street directory, whose own account of his ordeal among the American Indians had been dismissed as incredible. There were many reasons for public scepticism about Bruce's *Travels*. His descriptions of curious local customs outraged European standards of decency and undermined contemporary admiration for the 'Noble Savage'. The episode to which Kay's caption refers is a fair example: 'Not long after our losing sight of the ruins of this ancient capital of Abyssinia, we overtook three travellers driving a cow before them . . . We saw that our attendants attached themselves in a particular manner to the three soldiers that were driving the cow, and held a short conversation with them . . . The drivers suddenly tipt up the cow, and gave the poor animal

James Bruce of Kinnaird as the elegant grandee on the Grand Tour in 1762 by Pompeo Batoni. Bruce wrote to his fiancée, Margaret Murray of Polmaise: 'I begin sitting tomorrow to the best painter in Italy . . . and the miniature is to be copied from that picture by the best painter of miniatures in Italy, who is a lady. This is as certain a way of your having as good a picture as the subject will admit of.'

How dare you approach me with your travells. There is not a single word of them true
There you may be right, and altho I never dined upon the Lion or eat half a Cow and turned
the rest to grafs, yet my works have been of more use to mankind than yours
and there is more truth in one page of my Edin.ʳ directory than in all your five
Volumes 4.º. So when you talk to me dont imagine yourself at the source of the Nile!

I. Kay Del. et Sculp. Publifhed as the Act Directs 1791

Bruce's *Travels* were dismissed by most of his contemporaries as so many 'tall tales'. John Kay's satirical etching shows 'the Abyssinian' disputing with Peter Williamson who introduced the penny post to Edinburgh and compiled the city's first street directory. As a child Williamson had been sold into slavery in America where he was kidnapped and tortured by Indians.

a very rude fall upon the ground . . . One of them sat across her neck, holding down her head by the horns, the other twisted the halter about her forefeet, while the third, who had a knife in his hand, to my very great surprise, in place of taking her by the throat, got astride upon her belly before her hindlegs, and gave her a very deep wound in the upper part of her buttock . . . I let my people go forward, and staid myself, till I saw, with the utmost astonishment, two pieces, thicker, and longer than our ordinary beef steaks, cut out of the higher part of the buttock of the beast . . . and the two pieces were spread upon the outside of one of their shields.

One of them continued holding the head, while the other two were busied in curing the wound. This too was done not in any ordinary manner; the skin which had covered the flesh that was taken away was left entire; and flapped over the wound, and was fastened to the corresponding part by two or more small skewers, or pins . . . At the riverside where they were, they had prepared a cataplasm of clay, with which they covered the wound; they then forced the animal to rise, and drove it before them, to furnish them with a fuller meal when they should meet their companions in the evening . . .

When I first mentioned this in England, as one of the singularities which prevailed in this barbarous country, I was told by my friends that it was not believed. I asked the reason of this disbelief, and was answered, that people who had never been out of their own country, and others well acquainted with the manners of the world, for they had travelled as far as France, had agreed the thing was impossible, and therefore it was so . . . They suggested to me, in the most friendly manner, how rudely a very learned and worthy traveller had been treated for daring to maintain that he had eat part of a lion . . . They said, that, being convinced by these connoisseurs his having eat any part of a lion was *impossible*, he had abandoned this assertion altogether, and after only mentioned it in an appendix; and this was the farthest I could possibly venture.' This advice was disregarded in the interests of science and Bruce's self-respect. He also had to compete with the tremendous publicity surrounding Captain Cook's Pacific voyages and the Tahitian Omai whom Cook had brought back to London. Above all educated society resented Bruce's challenge to its idealistic vision of Abyssinia derived from the legends of Prester John and Dr Johnson's *Rasselas* (1759), an allegorical tale of an imaginary Abyssinian prince. Bruce's credibility was undermined still further by a snide remark from Johnson to the effect that when he 'first conversed with Mr Bruce, the Abyssinian traveller, he was very much inclined to believe that he had been there, but that he had afterwards altered his opinion.'

Although Bruce remained a laughing stock, his *Travels* – the first informed account of North Africa since the Jesuits – were still regarded as essential reading at the time of the British military expedition to Abyssinia in 1868. As Cook had publicised the South Seas, Bruce publicised Africa and twenty years later the African Association was founded for the systematic exploration of the continent. The Abyssinia of the *Travels* was sufficiently exotic and bizarre to inspire an entire literature from Coleridge's *Kubla Khan* to Rider Haggard. Bruce himself represented a transition between the enlightened traveller of the eighteenth century and the professional explorer of the nineteenth.

Captain Hugh Clapperton
1788–1827

Captain Hugh Clapperton RN, explorer of the Niger.

When Europe took up the challenge of Africa in the 1780s, public attention was naturally drawn to West Africa as the third corner of the Atlantic 'Slave Triangle'. The 'Slave Coast' became the starting-point for the exploration of the River Niger, the key to the economic penetration of West Africa. In 1795 the African Association sent out the first successful expedition to the Niger under the Selkirk surgeon Mungo Park whose exploits awakened government interest in the area. Opponents of slavery argued that the introduction of legitimate trade in goods such as cotton and palm oil might bring an end to the slave traffic by generating an alternative source of wealth.

Humanitarian and economic thinking prompted the government-subsidised expedition of 1823 which aimed to open up a route into the Western Sudan via Tripoli and Bornu. After the fall of Napoleon in 1815 naval officers and ships were made available for voyages of discovery. The most enterprising member of the 1823 expedition, Captain Hugh Clapperton, was a Lowlander from Annan in Dumfriesshire. As a boy he had been forcibly enlisted in the navy by the press-gang. During the Anglo-American war of 1812 he served in Canada where he planned to marry a Red Indian princess. Starting from Tripoli, Clapperton, Dixon Denham, an Army major, and Oudney, a naval surgeon, crossed the Sahara and discovered Lake Chad. Two years later Clapperton was authorised to establish trade relations with Sultan Bello of Sokoto, the dominant power in the Western Sudan. Civil war disrupted negotiations, the hoped-for treaty came to nothing and Clapperton himself died of dysentery in Sokoto. In 1830 his servant Richard Lander traced the course of the lower Niger. These expeditions solved the last major questions about the Niger and so completed the work begun by Mungo Park. By the 1840s British merchants had pioneered trade in the Niger delta, dealing in palm oil, used in the production of soap and candles, and palm kernels, the basis of the margarine industry developed in the 1870s. Initiatives of this kind were also supported by the evangelical advocates of legitimate trade who were lampooned by Dickens in *Bleak House*: like Mrs Jellyby they devoted themselves 'to an extensive variety of public subjects and especially to the subject of Africa with a view to the cultivation of the coffee berry, and a happy settlement of our superabundant population in Borrioboola-Gha on the left bank of the Niger'.

A Sidelong View of Africa: 'Timbuctoo'

The assault on the Niger begun by Park gathered momentum with the expeditions of Clapperton, rapidly followed by those of his fellow-Scot Major Gordon Laing and of René Caillié, both bound for the fabulous city of Timbuktu. By 1829 West Africa was in the headlines and the theme set for the annual poetry competition at Cambridge University that year was 'Timbuctoo'. The prize was won by the young Alfred Tennyson. A mock-heroic alternative by Thackeray appeared in a student magazine called *The Snob* with a footnote acknowledging the author's particular indebtedness to the *Travels* of Captain Hugh Clapperton.

> In Africa (a quarter of the world)
> Men's skins are black, their hair is crisp and curl'd;
> And somewhere there, unknown to public view,
> A mighty city lies, called Timbuctoo.
> There stalks the tiger, – there the lion roars
> Who sometimes eats the luckless blackamoors;
> All that he leaves of them the monster throws
> To jackals, vultures, dogs, cats, kites, and crows.
> His hunger thus the forest monarch gluts,
> And then lies down 'neath trees called cocoa-nuts.
> Quick issue out, with musket, torch, and brand,
> The sturdy blackamoors, a dusky band!
> The beast is found, – pop goes the musketoons, –
> The lion falls, covered with horrid wounds.
> At home their lives in pleasure always flow,
> But many have a different lot to know!
> They're often caught, and sold as slaves, alas!
> Thus men from highest joy to sorrow pass.
> Yet though thy monarchs and thy nobles boil
> Rack and molasses in Jamaica's isle!
> Desolate Afric! thou art lovely yet!
> One heart yet beats which ne'er shall thee forget.
> What though thy maidens are a blackish brown,
> Does virtue dwell in whiter breasts alone?
> Oh no, oh no, oh no, oh no, oh no!
> It shall not, must not, cannot, e'er be so.
> The day shall come when Albion's self shall feel
> Stern Afric's wrath, and writhe 'neath Afric's steel.
> I see her tribes the hill of glory mount,
> And sell their sugars on their own account;
> While round her throne the prostrate nations come,
> Sue for her rice and barter for her rum.

Capital of the gold trade in the great savanna empire of Mali, Timbuktu was a centre of Islamic culture and a no-man's land for the Western Christian. As such it had been one of the perennial legends of Africa since the Middle Ages. In time it became proverbial – a popular synonym for the 'back of beyond' – and one of many obsessions absorbed into the myth of the 'Dark Continent' which grew out of geographical ignorance, the common assumption of the innate superiority of

Western civilisation and the duty of the European to enlighten his racial and cultural inferior. This in turn gave moral sanction to colonisation and would be used to justify the questionable ambitions of later builders of Empire. The self-conscious humour of Thackeray's bad verse seems to mask a genuine if oblique challenge to the mentality of 1829.

Walter Montagu Kerr
1852–1888

Walter Montagu Kerr, explorer of Central Africa in the wake of Livingstone. 'There is a peculiar charm in the idea of being able to help in developing the resources of a country, to raise it from prostration, and to lighten the darkness, so that finally it may attain a position similar to that which is occupied by ourselves.'

AFRICAN MISSION

Livingstone's funeral in Westminster Abbey in 1874 sparked off a revolution. His 'martyrdom' in the cause of commerce and Christianity opened the floodgates to missionaries, prospectors and empire-builders eager to carry out or exploit his vision of the white man's contribution to the development of Africa. Walter Montagu Kerr, a grandson of the 6th Marquess of Lothian, was typical of the younger generation who shared Stanley's ambition of becoming 'the next martyr to geographical science'. Kerr's solitary trek from Cape Colony to the Lake regions of Central Africa (1883–85) was evidently modelled on Livingstone's transcontinental journey of 1853–56, a feat of endurance which had intoxicated the British public. Livingstone was the virtuoso solo traveller *par excellence* whose expeditions became the guage for measuring all later achievements and made Africa the ideal field for displays of lonely heroism.

Kerr aimed for the Scottish mission at Livingstonia, but found it deserted and was eventually rescued by a steamer of the African Lakes Company. Travelling at his own expense, Kerr was at heart a big game hunter (as he appears in the photograph by H S Mendelssohn of London, emerging from the bamboo jungle of the photographer's studio) who toyed with science and philanthropy. In his narrative *The Far Interior*, enthusiastic descriptions of game trophies mingle with observations on the East African slave trade – the Livingstone touch. He ends with a late Victorian appeal to Progress: 'Mayhap with the rise of an irresistible tide of progress the sun of prosperity may appear, dissolving the clouds of storm and strife from the face of this unhappy land, and shedding for ever a light of peace and joy, making the hitherto inaccessible home of the black man a World's Elysium.' The European 'Scramble for Africa' was just beginning.

'And he said unto them, Go ye into all the world, and preach the gospel to every creature.'
(Mark 16:15)

With the exception of Islam, no world religion has rivalled the burgeoning of the Christian movement for overseas mission at the turn of the last century. The most radical transformation took place in Africa where the idea of the 'Dark Continent' was a paradigm of European mission. In Africa extensive white penetration began with mission; in India, with trade.

The British movement emerged from the Evangelical Revival of the late eighteenth century and was also supported by devotees of the secular philosophy of Progress. It was spearheaded by the Baptists whose zeal was fired by Captain Cook's revelations of a new world in the Pacific. Missionary associations sprang up in quick succession, the most influential being the London Missionary Society (1795). In Scotland, which was feeling the impact of Wesley's preaching, the first societies were formed in Edinburgh and Glasgow. These were independent of the Church of Scotland which did not adopt an official policy of foreign mission until 1824. In its early stages African mission was closely linked with the campaign against the Atlantic slave trade, and Livingstone's famous slogan of 'commerce and Christianity' was derived from the abolitionists' championship of lawful commerce as a replacement for the traffic in 'black ivory'.

Superficially, the missionaries failed in their aim of mass conversion. Many were blinkered in their approach to native traditions, rigidly upholding the superiority of Western culture and never questioning their equation of European and true Christian values. Livingstone was an exception. By the late nineteenth century the public image of African mission had become tarnished. Livingstone's slogan had been altered to Rhodes's 'philanthropy plus five per cent' and missionary outreach was seen as an arm of Imperialist expansion. This did not invalidate the lasting achievements of Christian missionaries in medical care and education.

From Greenland's icy mountains,	Take up the White Man's burden –
From India's coral strand,	Send forth the best ye breed –
Where Afric's sunny fountains	Go bind your sons to exile
Roll down their golden sand,	To serve your captives' need;
From many an ancient river,	To wait in heavy harness,
From many a palmy plain,	On fluttered folk and wild –
They call us to deliver	Your new caught, sullen peoples,
Their land from error's chain . . .	Half devil and half child . . .
Can we, whose souls are lighted	Take up the White Man's burden –
With wisdom from on high,	And reap his old reward:
Can we to men benighted	The blame of those ye better,
The lamp of life deny?	The hate of those ye guard –
Salvation! oh, salvation!	The cry of hosts ye humour
The joyful sound proclaim,	(Ah, slowly!) towards the light: –
Till each remotest nation	'Why brought ye us from bondage,
Has learn'd Messiah's name.	Our loved Egyptian night?'
(Bishop Heber of Calcutta 1819)	(Rudyard Kipling)

Robert Moffat
1795–1883

Robert Moffat as he appeared at the time of Livingstone's funeral in the photograph by Elliott and Fry was the 'patriarch of South African missions whose thin benignant face is bronzed and his flowing beard whitened by 54 years of African labour'. A representative figure of early Victorian mission, he rose like Livingstone from the 'godly poor' of Scotland. Born in Ormiston, East Lothian, he worked as a gardener until 1815 when he came under the influence of the Wesleyan Methodists in Cheshire. In 1817 he was sent out to South Africa by the London Missionary Society to begin half a century of service.

Robert Moffat about 1870 – 'the patriarch of South African missions whose thin benignant face is bronzed and his flowing beard whitened by 54 years of African labour.'

From the outset he faced vigorous opposition from the British authorities in Cape Colony and the Boers, farmer-colonists of Dutch descent. On the northern boundary of the Colony along the Orange River dispossessed tribes and outlaws had been persuaded by missionaries to form the semi-independent Griqua republics, each with a missionary as adviser and diplomat. To curtail their political involvement the British Government had prohibited all missionary activity outside the Colony. By championing the rights of the Africans the London Society had also incurred the hatred of the Boers, whom they had deprived of a cheap source of labour and whose caste-like conception of Christianity excluded the equality of black and white. Only in 1821 was Moffat allowed to settle beyond the frontier in Bechuanaland. At Kuruman his doctrine of 'the Bible and the plough' was put into practice: efficient farming was introduced and a printing press for the publication of the first Sechuana edition of the Bible.

While on leave in London (1839–43) he had a momentous encounter with the young Livingstone whom he persuaded to opt for Africa. Moffat's outstanding achievement, the creation of the first white settlement in Central Africa, was completed at Livingstone's instigation. Since 1829 Moffat had cultivated a close friendship with the fiercest African chieftain of his time, Mzilikazi of the Matabele. As a result he was recognised as a power in the land, barring the steady northward advance of the trekking Boers. During the 1850s Livingstone built up a vision of the whole Zambesi basin as a Christian commonwealth headed by the Makololo and Matabele tribes. In pursuit of this idea the London Missionary Society dispatched two parties from Kuruman in 1859. The Makololo mission met with disaster. Moffat, on the strength of his personal prestige with Mzilikazi, was granted land for the other party in the first of a series of concessions which guaranteed British control over Rhodesia/Zimbabwe against the insistent pressure of the Boers.

'A Dumpy Sort of Man with a Bible Under His Arm'

Unlike Livingstone Moffat came near to fulfilling public expectations of the early Victorian missionary who saw his calling in the narrow sense of 'saving souls'. This curious portrait, painted in 1842 shortly before Moffat's return to Africa, shows him preaching to two black converts who had accompanied him to Britain in 1839. Moffat, who was a forceful personality and an imposing figure standing well over six feet, has been reduced to the popular image of the model missionary, scathingly characterised by Livingstone as 'a dumpy sort of man with a Bible under his arm'. Livingstone's private conception of building the Kingdom of God was far more demanding: 'I have laboured in bricks and mortar, at the forge and carpenter's bench, as well as in preaching and medical practice. I am "not my own". I am serving Christ when shooting a buffalo for my men, or taking an astronomical observation . . .' For Livingstone the explorer, 'serving Christ' also implied a response to the challenge of the unknown. The reality of African mission was an outright con-

Moffat as Apostle of the Bechuana.

tradiction of the popular ideal of 'sitting under a tree talking to a native' (Bishop Steere). Missionaries acquired temporal as well as spiritual authority: in practice converts tended to regard the missionary as their chief and all-provider who might be called upon for economic support, for the maintenance of law and order and, in the last resort, for military defence.

Moffat's portrait is essentially a piece of missionary propa-

Saint Peter preaching: detail from a fifteenth-century altarpiece by Fra Angelico.

ganda, owing much to popular prints with their 'before' and 'after' presentation of the African. This extract from *Blackwood's Magazine* of 1844 is typical of the 'before' presentation: 'This is Central Africa: distinguished from all the earth by the unspeakable mixture of squalidness and magnificence, simplicity of life yet fury of passion, savage ignorance of its religious notions yet fearful worship of evil powers, its homage to magic, and desperate beliefs in spells, incantations, and the fetish. The configuration of the country, so far as it can be conjectured, assists this primeval barbarism. The very fertility of the soil, at once rendering them indolent and luxurious [lascivious], excites their passions, and the land is a scene alike of profligacy and profusion.' The 'after' image stressed the convert's childlike innocence, gentleness and respect for the superior wisdom of the Western missionary. It also propagated the odd belief that Africans were somehow more susceptible to conversion than other non-Christian races.

In this portrait the artist has tried to reinforce the spiritual authority of the 'Apostle of the Bechuana' by making Moffat the focus of a design which is broadly related to earlier depictions of Christ or the Apostles preaching, as in this detail from a fifteenth-century altarpiece by Fra Angelico. As a gesture towards local colour he has also introduced into his idealised – or perhaps anglicised – African landscape an ox-wagon of the exact type used by the Boers and by South African missionaries.

David Livingstone
1813–1873

'I go back to Africa to make an open path for commerce and Christianity; do you carry out the work which I have begun.'

Livingstone's rallying cry to the Cambridge undergraduates in 1857 focused public attention on Africa as never before, arousing nationwide enthusiasm for overseas mission. He did not measure success by mass conversions: his ultimate aim was the regeneration of Africa through the impact of Western Christian civilisation as a whole and to this end he dedicated his life to the eradication of one of the main evils of African society, the slave trade.

The most influential and unorthodox missionary of the nineteenth century began life as a 'piecer' in a Blantyre cotton mill. In 1837 he was accepted by the London Missionary Society as a medical missionary. Debarred from going to China by the outbreak of the 'Opium War', he was recruited by his future father-in-law Robert Moffat for the Society's station at Kuruman in South Africa. In 1849 he made his debut as an explorer when he set out to extend the mission fields northward into the interior beyond the Kalahari desert. His successful location of the Zambesi river offered the prospect of a new route into Central Africa free from harassment by the hostile trekking Boers. Here he witnessed the devastating effects of slave raids. Livingstone's remedy was the promotion of 'commerce and Christianity' as the twin pioneers of civilisation: the Africans

David Livingstone at Hamilton in 1864 by
Thomas Annan – the most popular photograph
of the greatest of all Scottish missionaries.

were to learn how to pay for their imported European manufacturers with local produce instead of 'black ivory'.

The forging of a highway for lawful commerce called for a thorough exploration of the Zambesi basin and the transformation of Livingstone the missionary into a professional explorer. His strategy amounted to a one-man advance on the African interior. Travelling without European companions, he completed a coast to coast crossing of the continent in 1856. This epic achievement, including the discovery of the Victoria Falls, made him a national hero and set in motion a missionary invasion of an area previously known only to the Portuguese. The reluctance of the London Missionary Society to underwrite 'plans connected only remotely with the spread of the Gospel' and 'to enter upon untried, remote and difficult fields of labour' – ostensibly for financial but perhaps also for political reasons – determined Livingstone to sever his connection with the organized missionary movement and his next major expedition to the Zambesi (1858–64) was sponsored by the British government.

Livingstone's last fateful journey in search of the source of the Nile (1866–73) was arguably the most significant of all. His revelations about the horrors of the slave trade contained in the journals recovered by Stanley at Ujiji stirred the British government into decisive action and within a few months of his death the Sultan of Zanzibar abolished the Arab-controlled East African slave trade. The exploration of the Congo basin, begun shortly before Livingstone's death, was energetically pursued by Stanley, culminating in the foundation of the Belgian Congo. In East Africa the lucrative trade envisaged by Livingstone provoked international rivalries solved by outright territorial annexation. His greatest legacy was intangible – the goodwill towards the white man which he had inspired among Africans and the gradual revolution in European attitudes since 1866 when the *Anthropological Review* had dismissed his sympathetic views of the African as the fantasies of a 'poor naked mind bedaubed with the chalk and red ochre of Scotch theology, and with a threadbare, tattered waistcloth of education hanging around him.'

The Zambesi Expedition
1858–1864

Although Livingstone remained first and foremost a missionary, the Zambesi expedition marked a turning-point in his African service. His experience in the African interior had strengthened his resolve to close both the Portuguese and the Arab avenues of the slave trade by opening up the Zambesi as an artery for 'legitimate commerce'. In 1857 the British government, which stood to gain in popularity by supporting a national figure, invited Livingstone to lead an official expedition to the lower Zambesi, a fertile region also rich in minerals. His undivulged purpose was to plant a British colony in the highlands of Central Africa.

Above Tete Livingstone encountered an impassable gorge and a series of rapids which meant the end of the Zambesi as a

40

navigable channel from the coast to the interior highlands. Turning aside to investigate its main tributary the River Shire, he selected the Shire Highlands as the most favourable site for European settlement. Further to the north he sighted Lake Nyasa – a major discovery equalling that of Lake Tanganyika by Burton and Speke.

In other respects, however, the expedition was a comparative failure and in 1863 Livingstone was formally recalled as it was obvious that his exertions had helped to extend the catchment area of the Arab slavers. Having been unable to sell his steamer the *Lady Nyasa*, Livingstone was obliged to borrow his passage money to Britain, and did not reach London until July 1864. Although he was spared stringent criticism his popularity was at a low ebb. Nevertheless it was Thomas Annan's photograph, taken later that year in Hamilton where the Annans were neighbours of the missionary's sisters, which gained the widest circulation of all impressions of Livingstone. Prior to the Zambesi expedition he had been appointed roving consul to East Africa in order to impress his official status upon the Portuguese who dominated the area. He continued to wear his famous 'Consul's Cap' as a status symbol, valued for the prestige which it gave him with both Arab slavers and African tribesmen.

Livingstone's hopes of a British settlement were not realised: the government refused to be drawn into colonial adventures, at least for the moment. His death in 1873 supplied the emotional incentive for a national reappraisal of prospects in East Africa. In 1875 the Free Church founded a centre of commerce, civilisation and Christianity at Livingstonia on the shores of Lake Nyasa (Lake Malawi). The Church of Scotland followed with a rival memorial station in the Shire Highlands which was named after Livingstone's birthplace, Blantyre. In 1878 a group of Glasgow businessmen formed the African Lakes Company to ease the problems of communication and also 'to advance the kingdom of God by honest trade'. Tobacco and tea plantations were laid out and in 1889 the combined pressures of mission and trade persuaded the British government to declare a formal protectorate over Nyasaland. The nucleus of modern Malawi had been created in fulfilment of Livingstone's vision.

Private

River Shire, E.Africa
20. Oct. 1859

My Dear Sir William

Without making any apology for my long silence I shall begin by telling you that our prospects are beginning to brighten in a quarter that I never dreamed of. We have just traced this river up to its point of departure from the hitherto undiscovered Lake Nyasa and we found that there are only thirty three miles of cataracts when the river becomes smooth again and continues so right into Nyassa in 14°25′ South Lat. We have a channel of at least 2 fathoms from the sea at Kongone harbour up to 15°55′ S. Then 33 miles, and beyond that a region bathed by the river and Lake which really seems to be a finer cotton field than the American, for there are no frosts to endanger or cut off the crops and one sowing of foreign seed, already introduced by the natives themselves, serves for three years crops. Immediately beyond the cataracts the land East of Shire rises in three terraces of 1200 ft.–2000 ft. and 3000 feet respectively. These are abundantly supplied with running rills of delicious water, and cotton is now grown extensively on them all . . . On the other terraces it was delightfully cool though we were travelling in the hottest season of the year – that called in Western Africa 'the smokes', when from the burning of tens of thousands of acres of tall grass the atmosphere has somewhat the appearance of a London fog – there we have a country that would keep Europeans well, while one of the greatest benefits our expedition has to shew is the means of curing fever on the lowlands even, without in general, loss of strength to the patient. Well beyond this the land between Shire & the Lakes contracts into a narrow isthmus . . . All the slave & other trade from the Interior to the East coast must cross the isthmus in order to get past the Lakes without embarking on either – We met a large slaving party there with an immense number of slaves and elephants tusks. A more blackguard looking lot I never saw before. When they knew that we were English [sic] they slipped off by night . . . Now an English Establishment here for lawful commerce and with that gospel which is the only potent remedy for human woe and for raising degraded humanity would in the course of time be an incalculable boon to Africa and a benefit to England . . . The cotton trade would easily be developed for according to the Portuguese the people are quick of apprehension even when in a state of slavery – They are great cultivators and have no cattle – Some can see at a glance whither my efforts & aspirations tend. And perhaps the Good Lord may permit me the honour and privilege to open a door for the benefit of our own poor and to free our manufacturers from dependance on and encouragement of slave labour – Others think that I am following the glory of discovering lakes, mountains & Jenny nettles – 'Puir things they ken naething aboot it' . . . Believe me My Dear Friend I think a mission of our own honest Scottish poor will do more in this country than any other measure. There is room enough and to spare and they would shine as lights in the world and hold up their pastors hands when all the heathen are against him . . .

(Extract from a letter to the former Provost of Edinburgh, Sir William Johnston, in New College Library)

'Dr. Livingstone, I Presume?'

Stanley's comically restrained greeting to the 'lost' Livingstone became a favourite catchphrase of the late Victorians. Of all African explorers Livingstone alone was of sufficient stature to launch an obscure Welsh-American journalist on a great career. As self-promoted heir to Livingstone, Stanley embarked on a

42

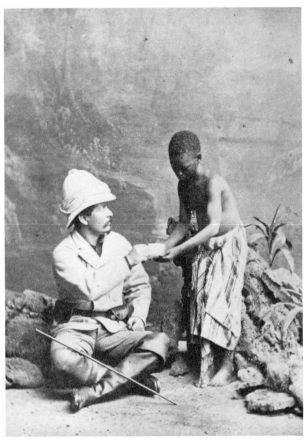

'Mr Stanley in the dress he wore when he met Livingstone', being offered refreshments by his valet Kalulu in the Darkest Africa of the photographer's studio.

Another photograph from the series commissioned by Stanley in 1872 to advertise himself as the 'discoverer' of Livingstone.

massive programme of exploration in the Congo Basin in 1874. Having failed to interest Britain in its economic potential, he turned to the African International Association patronised by Leopold II of Belgium as a cover for colonial ambitions. His next Congo journey of 1879 – the first overtly political expedition of the century – laid the foundations of the Congo Free State, nominally independent but actually a satellite of Belgium. Stanley had triggered off the 'Scramble' for tropical Africa.

In 1872 as part of his hectic campaign of self-advertisement Stanley posed for a highly popular series of carte-de-visite photographs by the London Stereoscopic Company which were designed as collectors' items for the mass market. In order to ensure maximum publicity the intrepid buccaneer had himself photographed in 'the dress he wore when he met Livingstone' and was accompanied by his valet Kalulu, a slave boy presented to him by an Arab trader on his expedition in search of Livingstone.

Reverend William Govan
1804–1875
and Reverend Ebenezer Miller
1799–1857

The earliest targets for British missions to Africa were Sierra Leone and Cape Colony, the latter being the nucleus of modern South Africa. In the West the missionary thrust was frustrated by the combined pressures of a hostile climate, the ever-present threat of malaria and the depredations of the Arab slavers, checked only by the coastal settlements of Europeans. In contrast the South with its healthier climate and flourishing settlements was a far more attractive prospect despite potential opposition from conservative colonial opinion, from marauding Bushmen to the north of the Colony and from the Bantu on the east who fiercely resisted European encroachment on their lands.

In the 1790s missionary attention was drawn to the Cape by developments in the Napoleonic wars. In 1795 Britain, already at war with France, automatically became the enemy of Holland when the Batavian Republic was established in the Netherlands under French auspices. A British force was shipped to the Cape and annexed the Colony, founded by the Dutch East India Company in the seventeenth century, in order to forestall French ambitions and to safeguard communications via the Cape with Britain's expanding Indian Empire. In 1802 the territory was restored to Holland, but on the resumption of hostilities it was retaken by Britain and the occupation was ratified at the Congress of Vienna in 1815. Missionaries followed the flag, led by the London Missionary Society and its Glasgow equivalent. Gradually the frontiers of European influence were extended beyond the Orange River as a 'Missionary Road' was forged into Central Africa. Of these pioneers the most distinguished were all Scots licensed by the London Society – John Philip, Moffat and Livingstone. Their efforts were backed by a host of lesser figures such as Ebenezer Miller, the head of a missionary training college in London affiliated to the London Missionary Society, who was received into the Free Church after the Disruption of the Church of Scotland and was posted to Cape Town.

The most far-reaching contribution made by the Glasgow Missionary Society was the creation of Lovedale (now part of the town of Alice), the most important of the British mission stations in South Africa. It was opened in 1824 by representatives of Dr John Love, a founder of the Glasgow Missionary Society, and had special emphasis on education. In 1841 it was transformed into a seminary and an ecumenical institute of higher education under the leadership of William Govan who had been ordained in Glasgow that year as missionary to the region of Kaffraria. Govan's policies were clearly shaped by the principles of the great Indian missionary Alexander Duff: education was to be in English in racially integrated classes – a policy unique to Lovedale – and was directed towards an African elite who would educate and convert the mass of the population as yet untouched by European evangelism. With government subsidies Govan developed vocational training and introduced a printing press for the publication of vernacular literature, as Moffat had done at Kuruman.

Reverend William Govan of Lovedale, the most important British mission station in South Africa, was photographed by D O Hill and Robert Adamson on his return to Scotland in 1846.

Reverend Ebenezer Miller of Cape Town with his family, a study by Hill and Adamson.

During the bloody Kaffir Wars of the 1840s and early 1850s the work of the institution was temporarily suspended. On the outbreak of war in 1846 Govan returned to Scotland where he was photographed by Hill and Adamson. Lovedale survived the devastation and Govan, after three years as minister of the Free Church congregation at Inchinnan, Renfrewshire, was reinstated as principal in 1850. Under his successor, James Stewart, Lovedale was chosen as the model for the Free Church station at Livingstonia. As in India the Church's greatest legacy was medical care and education: the missionary societies established schools all over South Africa for the teaching of basic literacy, simple hygiene and the elements of the Christian faith and in 1898 Lovedale became the site of the first mission hospital. Until the 1950s education continued to be Church-dominated, producing many leaders of post-colonial Africa such as Kenneth Kaunda of Zambia and Julius Nyerere of Tanzania.

'THAT LEGACY OF INSULT AND DIFFICULTY': THE 1868 CAMPAIGN IN ABYSSINIA

Before the travels of Bruce in 1769 European contact with Abyssinia/Ethiopia was negligible. From the Middle Ages Abyssinia haunted the European imagination as the kingdom of the mysterious Prester John and an island of Christianity within the Islamic empire of North Africa, ruled by a dynasty which claimed direct descent from a son of King Solomon by the Queen of Sheba. After sporadic cooperation with the Portuguese in the fifteenth and sixteenth centuries the country withdrew into its splendid isolation. Britain's interest in the Red Sea area was aroused by the Napoleonic campaigns which imperilled her vital communications with India. In 1848 Abyssinia relaxed its traditional policy of entrenched resistance to external influence in order to receive a British consul and a treaty of commerce was concluded.

In 1855 a guerrilla leader called Lij Kassa fought his way to the throne with a determination to reunite a country ravaged by generations of anarchy. He saw himself as a man of destiny dedicated to the eventual re-conquest of the whole non-Christian world and took the name of Theodore in fulfilment of an ancient prophecy predicting the coming of a national saviour of that name. In 1860 the British consul was murdered. The emperor avenged his death by a massacre and approached Queen Victoria with an embarrassing request for military support on his great crusade against the Moslems. Diplomatic silence enraged Theodore who suspected the British of intriguing with his enemies in Egypt. The new consul was thrown in prison, followed by the French envoy and European missionaries. Britain, increasingly conscious of her imperial dignity, was outraged by the insolence of such an outlandish and petty princeling but reluctant to meet the risk and the expense of military action. The final provocation was the imprisonment of the British representative sent to negotiate with Theodore.

Theodore's defeat was not a foregone conclusion. Although most of the country was in revolt against his cruelties, he managed to retreat to his near impregnable rock fortress of Magdala. The storming of Magdala (which ended in his suicide) was a victory for British expertise and an impressive demonstration of imperial might: 'Princes and potentates scattered far apace heard the noise of it and trembled' (H M Stanley). In 1872 the Prince of Tigré emerged as the new ruler of Abyssinia after a long interval of civil strife. Britain refrained from political intervention but her recent military success fired the ambitions of other colonial powers. In 1896 Italian invaders were routed at Adowa. This did little to check European penetration in general and in 1935 an Italian protectorate was declared by Mussolini. It lasted until 1941 when Haile Selassie regained the throne, only to be overthrown by a military coup in 1974.

Robert, 1st Lord Napier of Magdala
1810–1890

Robert, 1st Lord Napier of Magdala, supreme commander on the Abyssinian campaign of 1868.

From the eighteenth century India received a steady influx of Scots in search of fame and fortune in the employment of the East India Company. Napier's career began in Bengal as a sapper trained by the Company. Distinguished service in the Sikh wars of 1845 and 1848 secured him an appointment as civil engineer to the British regency in the annexed province of the Punjab. His real chance came with the eruption of the Indian Mutiny in 1857. Under Sir James Outram he was entrusted with engineering operations before the capture of Lucknow and served with Sir Hugh Rose in the final drive against the mutineers. In 1860 he was promoted divisional commander under Sir James Hope Grant in the war in China which first brought Gordon of Khartoum into the headlines. From 1865 he commanded the Bombay Army in the province of Sind with special responsibility for the security of the North-West frontier.

Napier's Indian experience made him an ideal choice for the leadership of the 1868 mission to Abyssinia which faced extraordinary strategic problems, some of which were generated by the sheer scale of the British expedition. The chief advocates of the use of force against Emperor Theodore were officers of the Indian army who had been convinced by their experience of the Mutiny of the value of a sharp military lesson for rebellious natives. Since 1857 India had become the biggest single responsibility of the British army and the pick of its regiments were stationed there. Napier's force included a detachment of Bombay troops renowned for their hardiness and ability to withstand hot climates.

After the fall of Magdala Napier found himself a popular hero. The public was captivated by the exotic setting of the campaign, national honour had been satisfied, and Britain's status as an international military power had been restored after being challenged in the Crimea. For his brilliant success in Abyssinia Napier was raised to the peerage and given the supreme command in India.

King Theodore II of Abyssinia
1818–1868

The Noble Savage of the 1860s, the notorious Emperor Theodore II of Abyssinia – a carte-de-visite portrait by Neurdein of Paris.

In the 1850s the improvement of photographic techniques led to the introduction of cheap portrait photographs as a supplement to printed visiting cards. Photography with its new mass appeal gradually replaced miniature painting in response to popular demand for small portraits of family, friends and the famous. By the 1860s the word 'cartomania' had been coined to describe the craze for collecting these miniature photographs, mounted in special albums like stamps or cigarette cards. Cartes-de-visite were sold by stationers and publishers as well as photographers – Neurdein was a publisher specialising in historical portraits.

This souvenir portrait of Theodore, a sensational figure in the 1860s, was probably issued posthumously and is a strange blend of myth and realism. The meticulous accuracy of the costume and hair-style indicates that the artist must have had access to illustrations or photographs taken on the actual campaign. At the same time it is a romantic and idealised image overlaid with a suggestion of the theatre or of opera. It is literary. The fabulous empire of Prester John and the fictional Abyssinia of Dr Johnson were not entirely forgotten by 1868 and Disraeli could still announce that 'we have hoisted the standard of St George on the mountains of Rasselas'. Behind this portrait lies the tradition of the 'Noble Savage', the exotic hero who became a stock figure in eighteenth-century literature. The peak of his popularity coincided with the cult of nature and Cook's voyages to the South Seas when Europe discovered in Tahiti a new Eden. This idolisation of the 'Noble Savage' owed much to the social and political theories of Jean-Jacques Rousseau for whom (European) civilisation was an inevitable source of moral degradation. The American Indian, the Polynesian, and later the African, represented man in his primitive and uncorrupted state living in perfect harmony with his environment. Variations and mis-interpretations of Rousseau's estate of nature' persisted well into the nineteenth century, often conflicting with the first-hand experience of explorers and missionaries. Theodore was an example of this ambivalence: a Christian and a 'savage', the heir to the empire of Prester John and a capricious fanatic notorious for his atrocities. After his death a pen-picture in a leading article in *The Times* confirmed his apotheosis as the Noble Savage of the Victorian era:

'In his wildest freaks of passion, even in his savage brutalities, there was a singular consistency. He was of the stuff of which many an Eastern conqueror has been made. Endowed with an intense personal will, great courage, and wide designs, he was yet incapable of self-control, and wholly unable to understand the power of a civilisation higher than his own. Unhappily for himself he provoked a conflict with the arms of the West; he was unjust and violent and cruel in his injuries to unoffending subjects of the British Crown, he put our messengers of peace in chains, he misunderstood our forbear-ance, he challenged us to vindicate the wrongs we had suffered; yet it must be said of this self-proclaimed descendant of

Solomon, that, passionate and resolute to the end, he still fought when fighting was hopeless, and, as we may believe, preferred to die by his own hand rather than fall under the vengeance of an unknown enemy.'

(*The Times* 27 April 1868)

Abyssinia on Record: Pioneer Photographs by The Royal Engineers

The 1850s saw the advent of the first official war photographers, special correspondents and pictorial journalists representing the new illustrated journals. The Crimean War of 1854 set a precedent for all subsequent war reporting when, for the first time, correspondents, war artists and photographers from all over Europe converged on the scene of action. Among them were the famous William Howard Russell of *The Times*, Roger Fenton, the painter and founder of the Photographic Society of London, and a detachment of official photographers attached to the 77th Regiment who were unfortunately lost during a hurricane off Balaclava. Official promotion of photography as an aid to documentation continued during the Mutiny in India where Felice Beato (qv) was employed by the British War Office.

In 1856 the Royal Engineers set up a small photographic unit at their headquarters in Chatham which was intended to provide a photocopying service for the duplication of maps and plans. Following the successful deployment of military photographers during the American Civil War, the British Government decided to employ the same technique in Abyssinia. The British expeditionary force of 1868 had to negotiate some four hundred miles of the wildest and most inhospitable terrain they had ever encountered. Much of the territory on their route was unsurveyed and they had to rely on rough maps drawn on location. One non-commissioned officer and six men assigned to the 10th Company Royal Engineers produced an astonishing total of fifteen thousand photographic copies in the course of the campaign – and that in spite of the exceptional difficulties of transporting cumbersome and vulnerable equipment on pack mules. Their problems were increased by their dependence on the collodion or 'wet-plate' process which involved the manipulation of a glass plate in a wet condition throughout the operation. A portable dark-room – in this case, a tent – was essential as the plate had to be dipped in a sensitizing bath, exposed in the camera while still wet and then immediately removed and the negative image developed before the sensitizing chemicals could deteriorate.

The Engineers did not restrict themselves to their official function and took some sixty or seventy views of landscape and architecture along the entire line of the march from Zula to Magdala, sometimes at the instigation of their commanding officers who understood little or nothing about photography: 'Sometimes the mules had to be halted and the boxes unpacked during a long march in a drizzling rain in order that a picture might be attempted of some mountain or other, the top of which

48

was enveloped in a dense fog, simply because a staff officer had expressed himself to the effect that the whole would make a grand picture' (*The Photographic Journal* 15 December 1868). Portrait lenses were also carried and a favourite subject was the heir to the Abyssinian throne, Theodore's six-year-old son. After the fall of Magdala in April 1868 Dejatch Alamayou ('I have seen the world') and his mother appealed for British protection. When the queen died during the return march across Abyssinia Alamayou was adopted by Queen Victoria, whose generosity towards orphaned and dispossessed princes was unfailing. He was educated first at the Mission College in Bombay by the Reverend Dr John Wilson (qv) and then at Cheltenham College and Rugby. In 1879 after a year's training at Sandhurst he died prematurely of pneumonia. The more competent of the photographs taken by the Royal Engineers were reproduced as line engravings in the *Illustrated London News* and in the autumn of 1868 a whole series was exhibited to the public in London.

Ronald Leslie Melville, Amateur War Photographer and Correspondent

Dejatch Alamayou, orphaned son of Emperor Theodore and a protégé of Queen Victoria. One of *The Times* correspondents reported: 'He is a fine intelligent little fellow of seven years, with good brow and eyes but thick lips and corresponding chin. I saw him dressed with sword and shield at Ashangi, being photographed by the Royal Engineers, and he seemed especially delighted at some artillery practice that was going forward at the time close by.'

'I send you, dear Alfred, a complete photographic apparatus which will amuse you doubtless in your moments of leisure, and if you could send me home, dear, a good view of a nice battle, I should feel extremely obliged. P.S. If you could take the view, dear, just in the moment of victory, I should like it all the better.'

When the new art of photography was adopted as a fashionable pursuit, this apocryphal letter from a young lady to her fiancé in the Crimea appeared in *Punch*, satirising the growing enthusiasm for photographing battlefields as a novel form of tourist attraction on the Grand Tour of Europe and later in more exotic locations. Of the three photographs illustrated, two (the vignette of Dejatch Alamayou and the portrait group of soldiers at Magdala) were almost certainly taken by the Royal Engineers and were collected for a personal photograph album of miscellaneous family portraits and travel souvenirs by Ronald Leslie Melville, later 11th Earl of Leven (1835–1906). In later years the 11th Earl seems to have followed a fairly conventional career in banking and a succession of prestigious public offices including that of High Commissioner of the General Assembly of the Church of Scotland. Privately, however, he was a prolific and talented amateur photographer and watercolourist whose passion for photography and field-sports was shared by his great friend, the exiled Maharajah Duleep Singh (qv). In the 1850s and early 1860s several photographic societies were founded in London and the provinces. Melville joined the most exclusive of these, the Amateur Photographic Association which was established in 1861 under the presidency of the Prince of Wales.

The prospect of big-game hunting in Abyssinia and the chance to obtain photographs of a remote and virtually uncharted country must have proved irresistible for Ronald Leslie Melville. The international Press was out in force and, according to

Napier's troops posing by the Kafir Bur Gate at Magdala after the storming of Theodore's mountain fortress in April 1868. The picture was probably taken by the Royal Engineers.

A keen amateur photographer throughout his life, the 11th Earl of Leven went out to Abyssinia in 1868 as a war correspondent. At the telegraph office in Senafé he 'found a photo^c dark tent and a Mr. Brown the owner. Very civil and we organised a matinee photographique, beginning with the prisoners in the stocks. His being wet collodion, very successful; the brutes moved during my long dry plate exposure.'

family tradition, he secured access to Abyssinia as one of several war correspondents covering the 1868 campaign for *The Times*. Having sailed from Britain in January 1868, he toured the sites of Egypt where he witnessed the construction of the Suez Canal. In late February he reached the British base-camp at Zula, by which time the advance guard of the Army had already forged its way several hundred miles along the arduous route to Magdala. Melville's progress was slow and intermittently frustrated by official prohibitions to proceed to the front. Finally, in early April, he reluctantly decided to turn back: he did not expect to arrive in time for the finale at Magdala and in addition he must have been anxious to return to the coast before the rains commenced, making the intervening country almost impassable.

For the greater part of the journey Melville kept a detailed personal diary. This is a fascinating miscellany of humorous and often caustic character sketches, purple passages describing the Abyssinian landscape and the wildlife which he shot and prepared for taxidermy, apparently for his own private collection, and laconic notes on the problems of photography, interspersed with passing observations on the development of the campaign. Given that most amateur war photographs date from the late nineteenth century when technical advances made photography a less formidable undertaking, Melville's surviving photographs are quite remarkable and, in combination with his journal, present a compelling informal conspectus of the 1868 expedition. His racy accounts of incidents during the march are particularly absorbing, one of the best being that of an unexpected confrontation with the brother of Dejatch Kassai, the pro-British ruler of the province of Tigré who succeeded Emperor Theodore in 1872.

'April 7 . . . At Muski [or Muzgee] found Cassai's brother encamped with his army. I put on my sword, and yellow and red silk handkf. Luckily had on my short top boots, red striped stockings showing between them and my knickerbockers, and with a revolver and big knife, I was a striking object to a savage. In this get-up I marched alone through his camp and up to his tent . . . He was sitting in state on a hearth rug, with about 18 gentlemen in waiting and seemed delighted to see me, and made me sit on the rug by him. The gents in waiting stood or sprawled on the floor. The Chief is not a beauty, but very intelligent-looking; and the whole party had a well-bred look about them and some were really handsome . . . At first my visit was a little like the same ceremony in London. Having at his request sat down (we shook hands first), the conversation was a little inclined to flag, so I by wiping my face and fanning myself, remarked that it was a hot day – a dreadful truism which he was too well-mannered to show up, but softened as well as he could by giving me to understand that the novelty of the remark pleased him and that now I mentioned it, he really thought it was hot. Any English thermometer must have burst in the temperature of that tent. He then asked to look at my sword and expressed his satisfaction with it, and asked to see my revolver. Not wishing any savage to have it out of my hands, I showed him instead the knife Ld. Middleton gave me. The big blade with the spring to keep it open and the corkscrew particularly pleased him, but the lancet sent him into raptures and he exclaimed 'Christian, Christian, taib, taib' (= 'Christian, Christian, all right, all right'). At first I was at a loss to know what my possessing a lancet had to do with our religion, so he showed me that all his men, as well as wearing the blue string round their necks (sign of Xtianity), had also crosses tattoed on their arms, and he concluded my lancet could be for no other purpose than that of tattoing and marking Xtians . . . I gave him a penny looking-glass; it pleased him, but he had evidently seen them before. I luckily had a 6d. squeaking india-rubber doll in my pocket and gave my coat a squeeze which produced a slight squeak. He could not think where the sound came from. I gave it another and he thought I had a bird and was immensely amused when a doll representing an Englishwoman with gigantic crinoline and pork-pie hat appeared. His attendants crowded so close round to see this wonder of art, that I nearly died of the heat and smell of ghee [clarified butter] and each attendant in turn insisted on giving it a separate squeeze of his own . . . He then smoked a pipe of mine which nearly made him sick, and after that I took my leave. We shook hands, I believe with mutual hopes that we might meet again.'

BRITAIN AND THE SUDAN

Official British interest in Egypt dated from the Napoleonic campaign of 1798. Successive governments were obsessed by the fear that communications with British India might be jeopardised if Egypt – which was part of the Ottoman (Turkish) Empire – came under the influence of another European power. During the 1850s Egypt attracted substantial European investment, at first without political repercussions. British thinking was summarised by Palmerston in 1857: 'We do not want to *have* Egypt. We want to *trade* with Egypt . . . but we do not want the burthen of governing Egypt'. In 1876, however, the escalation of Egypt's foreign debt led to the institution of Anglo-French financial control. In 1882 the Khedive of Egypt was overthrown by an army coup provoked by strong resentment of both European and Turkish rule. To safeguard her own financial interests and the newly-built Suez Canal, Britain was forced into military intervention with the aim of restoring the discredited Egyptian authorities. The extended British occupation of Egypt was to act as a catalyst in the European 'Scramble for Africa'.

British hopes of a rapid withdrawal were shattered by the outbreak of a revolt in the Sudan, the hinterland of Egypt, which threatened Egyptian control over the area. Fired by militant nationalism and Islamic religious fervour, the rising was led by the Mahdi, a self-styled national saviour equally fanatical in his hatred of the Egyptians and the laxity of local religious practice. In 1883 a British force sent to protect Khartoum, the Sudanese capital, was massacred by the Mahdist rebels. In its anxiety to find a non-interventionist and relatively inexpensive but face-saving solution, Gladstone's government turned to General Gordon as former Governor-General of the Sudan. No military support was forthcoming as the government overlooked or chose to ignore the need for a political settlement. Gordon, who drastically underestimated the scale of the revolt, relied on his supposed influence in the Sudan and ordered the evacuation of the Egyptian garrisons. By March 1884 he was besieged in Kartoum. A relief force finally arrived in January 1885 to find Gordon dead and Khartoum in the hands of the Mahdi. In spite of the hysteria which followed Gordon's death

General Charles George Gordon
1833–1885

the Mahdi remained unchallenged until 1898 when he was crushed by Kitchener at the battle of Omdurman.

Gordon of Khartoum, religious extremist and political gadfly, was born into a Scottish family with strong military traditions. During the Crimean War he served with distinction as a junior officer of the Royal Engineers and in 1860 was posted to China where an Anglo-French force was 'encouraging' the Manchu Emperor to observe treaties opening Chinese ports to European trade. Within two years China was engulfed in the civil war known as the Taiping rebellion, a movement of religious protest directed against the Manchu dynasty and traditional Confucian culture. When the rebels threatened the international treaty port of Shanghai the European powers abandoned their stance of neutrality. British naval operations were backed by a small land force which had been nicknamed 'the Ever Victorious Army' and consisted of some two thousand Chinese soldiers of fortune headed by European officers. Under Gordon's command the motley Army, in cooperation with the Chinese authorities, contributed immeasurably to the eventual victory of the Imperial forces and Gordon was invested with the rare honour of the Yellow Jacket by the Emperor. The British government was, however, less enthusiastic: Gordon had been the focus of a diplomatic row and had wilfully disobeyed orders to cease operations against the rebels. Although the British Press discovered 'Chinese Gordon', he was given an obscure assignment on his return, building forts in the mouth of the Thames. Failure to secure a more challenging commission convinced Gordon of official displeasure and he devoted himself to social work as a champion of the ragged school movement.

After years of frustration in the British army Gordon took service with Khedive Ismail, the ruler of Egypt, in 1874. Ismail, who was pursuing a policy of Egyptian expansion in the Sudan, was trying to enlist British support by campaigning against the Arab-controlled slave trade – the basis of the country's economy. As Governor of Egyptian Equatoria on the Upper Nile (1874–6) Gordon put an end to the use of the Nile for slave traffic and set up a coherent administration. Back in Britain he found himself famous: missionary work, exploration and propaganda issued by the Anti-Slavery Society had stimulated popular interest in Central Africa. Since no government appointment was available, Gordon returned to the Khedive as Governor-General of the Sudan, only to resign in disgust over European interference in its internal affairs. Gordon was one of the earliest supporters of the concept of 'the white man's burden' or Imperialism as the moral duty of the 'haves' to serve the 'have nots', and the ultimate aim of his administration had been self-determination for the Sudan.

The choice of Gordon for the 1884 mission to the Sudan rested mainly on his personal charisma, first displayed in China. 'Chinese Gordon' could be presented to the public as a super-human figure if circumstances demanded it. His potential for

IN MEMORIAM

1885

A memorial portrait of General Gordon. 'His life was England's glory,/His death was England's pride.' (Popular song.)

The Cult of Gordon

The tragedy at Khartoum reconstructed in a famous painting by George William Joy.

martyrdom was fully realised in the tragedy at Khartoum, to the lasting dismay of Gladstone's government which had ignored his controversial advice to 'smash' the Mahdi.

'Too late! Too late to save him,
In vain, in vain, they tried.
His life was England's glory,
His death was England's pride.'

(Popular song)

For nearly six months Gladstone resisted growing pressure to send a force to Khartoum. Eventually public agitation became so intense that the government was obliged to discount the risk of extending British political responsibilities to the Sudan and reluctantly authorised an expedition in August 1884. Gordon's death unleashed a torrent of criticism: the government was charged with killing Gordon through incompetence and delay – a view shared by Queen Victoria herself – and Gladstone, the 'Grand Old Man' of Liberalism, was dubbed 'Murderer of Gordon'. The furore helped to precipitate the downfall of the Liberal administration and lasted for an entire generation.

The fate of 'Chinese Gordon' fostered one of the most inflated legends of the British Empire, provoking a national orgy of sentimentality and self-reproach. Events at Khartoum were elevated into a contemporary Passion Play with the hero cast in the role of popular saint, Christian martyr and beau idéal of the imperial soldier and administrator. The cult of Gordon was nourished by a spate of sermons, tracts, outpourings of moral

indignation, adventure stories, bad verse and 'Golden Gleanings from the Thoughts of General Gordon', and by the foundation of Gordon clubs and boys' homes financed by public subscription. Feelings ran so high that the manufacturers of Eno's Fruit Salts thought to boost their sales by consciously appealing to popular outrage over the inglorious relief expedition to the Sudan.

The Gordon literature was complemented by a whole iconography of martyrdom. In Lowes Dickinson's memorial portrait Gordon has been immortalised as the 'Warrior of God' and martyr to the British cause, symbolised by the Union Jack in the background of the picture. Gazing into the distance in tragic resignation across the beleaguered walls of Khartoum, he holds the field-glasses with which he has vainly scanned the horizon for the British relief expedition. His heroic status is emphasised by the draping of his cloak to recall statues of Roman emperors.

George William Joy's famous reconstruction of the tragedy was another monument of the campaign for 'avenging Gordon' which continued unabated into the 1890s. The painting was exhibited in 1894 with a dramatic quotation from Gordon: 'Now mark this, if the Expeditionary Force – and I ask for no more than 200 men – does not come in ten days, the town may fall; and I have done my best for the honour of our country. Goodbye. – C. G. Gordon, 14th December, 1884.' The reconquest of the Sudan by Kitchener in the 'River War' of 1896 was generally interpreted as a posthumous justification of Gordon's sacrifice. An idealised Gordon became the 'patron saint' of the new Anglo-Egyptian state and a Gordon Sunday was observed every January to commemorate his death.

India

THE BUILDING OF A BRITISH EMPIRE

'Civil war in a native kingdom is a sure sign that that kingdom will be shortly drawn irresistibly to that great magnetic power the East India Government. One by one the native princes fall like flies into the widespread web of the great benevolent spider of Leadenhall Street.'

(Illustrated London News 1856)

Until 1858 British India was ruled by the English India Company, a commercial corporation which operated under increasing interference from the British Crown. When it was chartered in 1600 the Company was a purely commercial venture without a political dimension. By the early 1700s it had coastal trading factories in Madras and Bengal and also in Bombay which had entered British possession as part of the dowry of Charles II's Portuguese queen, Catherine of Braganza.

The catalyst of change was activated by the decline of the Mughal dynasty in India, founded in 1526 by a direct descendant of the Mongol conquerors Tamburlaine and Genghis Khan. As a result of the collapse of centralised Mughal authority in the first decades of the eighteenth century the Company fortified its settlements and entered local politics: bona fide traders became armed traders and political agents, backed by a defensive army. The eclipse of the Mughals coincided with the emergence of France as a formidable commercial and colonial rival in India, transforming the role of the East India Company. Franco-British enterprise concentrated on the weakest points of the decaying empire in the South-East and Bengal. In 1756 Robert Clive's victory over the Nawab of Bengal at Plassey established British ascendancy in the province and by the 1760s serious French competition could be discounted. The Company was now a political powerhouse and had developed a system of 'masked government' which enabled it to govern through a puppet regime headed by a native ruler.

Vigorous expansion continued and the politicisation of the Company accelerated following the institution of a royal Governor-General of India in 1773. In 1784 State intervention increased with Pitt's creation of a Board of Control to scrutinise the Company's affairs. The right to appoint civil servants and cadets for the Company armies – one in each of the British dominions of Bengal, Bombay and Madras – was retained by the Company. The tremendous influx of Scots into India during this period was partly due to Scottish directorship of the Company and also to the presence of the Earl of Melville on the Board of Control. Demands for Company personnel helped to relieve social pressures in Britain as India became a mecca for younger sons and social misfits hoping to enjoy old age as managers or shareholders of the Company.

By the turn of the eighteenth century commercial and military opportunism had taken their toll and only three major states – Rajputana, Sind and the Sikh Punjab – remained intact. After a temporary lull during the Napoleonic wars empire-building resumed under a new stimulus, the fear of Russian expansion in Central Asia. The conquest of Sind by General Napier (1843) and the annexation of the Punjab (1849) extended the British Empire to the country's natural frontiers in the North-West. In the 1850s the policies of the Marquess of Dalhousie led to the absorption of most of the autonomous states, provoking the eruption of the Indian Mutiny in 1857. The Mutiny, which resulted in the abolition of East India Company government and its replacement by Crown rule, marked a watershed in the history of British India. Britain became acutely conscious of the pivotal economic and military position of her Indian Empire and the security of the routes to India was to act as a powerful incentive to British involvement in the partition of Africa.

Gilbert Elliott, 1st Earl of Minto
1751–1814

In 1807 Gilbert Elliott, created Earl of Minto in 1813, became the first Scot to hold the highest office in British India. The eldest son of the third baronet of Minto in Roxburghshire, the new Governor-General had first developed a connection with India in the 1780s when he prepared the case for the impeachment of Warren Hastings in collaboration with Burke, and this had been cemented by his appointment as President of the Board of Control for India.

By 1807 India was beginning to be recognised as the cornerstone of British wealth and status in the world as a whole. From the mid-eighteenth century the Anglo-French struggle for supremacy in the Indian Ocean had reinforced the gradual politicisation of the East India Company and formal empire was spreading towards the North-West mountain frontier of the sub-continent. In foreign policy Minto's prime objective was to outmanoeuvre French colonial initiatives in India and ultimately to achieve a total eradication of French influence from the eastern hemisphere. Whereas at the beginning of his term of office Britain was haunted by the dread of a Napoleonic invasion of her Indian Empire, by the end France had lost all her dominions east of the Cape of Good Hope – the Moluccan Islands, Bourbon/Réunion and Mauritius. Minto explained his strategy in a letter to his wife in 1810: 'I am just sending an expedition to make the conquest of the Isle of Bourbon . . . I propose to follow up the blow by attacking the Mauritius, generally called the Isle of France. These two acquisitions will be of extreme importance;

While George Chinnery strove to portray the Earl of Minto with the utmost panache as Governor-General of India, Sir Walter Scott remembered him as the Border laird and the private man: 'Sir Gilbert was indeed a man among a thousand. I knew him very intimately in the beginning of the century and, which was very agreeable, was much at his house on very easy terms. He loved the Muses and worship'd them in secret and used to read some of his poetry which was but middling.'

they are the only French possessions east of the Cape, and furnish the only means our arch-enemy can command for annoying us in this quarter of the world, till an army can come here in its shoes. From the Isle of France all the cruisers have been sent out against our trade; against which a very large squadron have done little to protect us. The losses of the Company, as well as the general trade, have been enormous . . .' These conquests were supplemented in 1811 by that of Java, headquarters of the Dutch East India Company and a prized possession of France's satellite, the Dutch Batavian Republic.

Minto's other Imperial adventures were mainly restricted to embassies to Persia, Lahore and Kabul in 1808 with a view to a defensive alliance against France, and the conclusion of a treaty of friendship with Sind. In British eyes his domestic policies were more controversial, giving rise to the so-called 'Battle of the Missions'. William Carey's missionaries at Serampore had used their printing press to issue tracts calculated to offend the Hindu population. This led the government to impose censorship in accordance with the Company's principles of religious tolerance in order to preserve peace, stability and commercial prospects within British territory. A pamphlet war ensued in Britain and Minto was accused of trying to hinder the spiritual enlightenment of heathen India. He was finally relieved of office in 1813 against the wishes of the Company to make way for the Earl of Moira, a personal friend of the Prince Regent.

An Imperial Portrait

' . . . Of the merits of the Work as far as it is a good resemblance of your Lordship I am well aware – many of the details were I believe very well – but I doubt whether in general Splendour and Effect it will keep pace with similar Works of Art at home at all . . .'

(Letter from George Chinnery 12 July 1814: Minto Papers in the National Library of Scotland)

In his apologetic letter to the Earl of Minto Chinnery took care to emphasise the lack of stimulus and competition from other artists as a factor bearing on the uneven quality of his own work. George Chinnery (1774–1852) was one of many British artists who went to India – Chinnery in fact became a permanent expatriate – in search of exotic motifs for landscape painting or portrait commissions from the wealthy clientele of native princes and socially ambitious officials of the East India Company. Others welcomed the opportunity to avoid unfavourable comparisons with superior painters at home. Chinnery sailed for India in 1802 after the apparent breakdown of his marriage and was soon well established as a portrait painter in Madras and Calcutta through the connections of the family firm of Chase, Sewell & Chinnery in Madras. Increasing success earned him commissions from two successive Governors-General, the Earls of Minto and Moira, and induced Chinnery to live beyond his means. In 1818 he was joined by his estranged wife but in 1825 he fled from debts and family to settle in China.

While in Calcutta Chinnery painted five portraits of the Earl of Minto. The one illustrated here was painted in 1812–13 as a private commission from the sitter who took it back to Scotland on his departure from India and whose family later presented it to the town of Hawick. A larger version was sent to Sir Stamford Raffles, the Governor of Java appointed by Minto. For all his apologies, Chinnery exerted himself to create a powerful image of Imperial dignity with all the panoply and rhetoric of a royal portrait in the tradition of Van Dyck. Maps of Java, Bourbon and Mauritius stress Minto's achievements as an empire-builder. These accessories of conquest are balanced by a group of symbolic statuary on the right of the picture. An Achilles-like male figure personifying War gazes down on two female figures who probably represent Prudence with a mirror and a serpent. One figure leans on the column of Constancy and Fortitude, while at her feet is a tamed lion associated with good government – a wide spectrum of rather indeterminate allegorical references.

Sir David Baird
1757–1829

Sir David Baird sketched by Sir David Wilkie for a painting commissioned by the General's widow in 1838.

David Baird, a younger son of the Bairds of Newbyth, was born in the year of Clive's victory at the battle of Plassey which established British ascendancy over Bengal. At sixteen he joined the army and in 1779 sailed for India as captain of the 73rd regiment in the pay of the East India Company. From the mid-to the late eighteenth century career prospects in the Company attracted a growing number of enterprising military Scots like Baird, other outstanding examples being Sir Hector Munro who captured the French trading post and power base of Pondicherry, Sir Eyre Coote and Sir John Malcolm (qv).

Baird's career in India followed the pattern of the Mysore wars against a background of Anglo-French commercial and territorial rivalries and the increasingly political manoeuvres of the East India Company. On arrival he fought in the 1780 campaign against Hyder Ali of Mysore, was taken prisoner and spent almost four years in captivity. Mysore, which was defended by the best equipped and best disciplined of all Indian armies, was a French-oriented but fiercely independent state in the South Indian hills and as such a constant menace to British supremacy. Hyder Ali and his son Tipu were exceptional among Indian rulers in their uncompromising resistance to any form of 'masked government' by the East India Company whether through alliance or subsidy.

Following his release Baird returned to India in 1791 to take part in the renewed conflict with Tipu, who had resolved on a 'holy war' against the infidel British to regain the territory lost by his father in the 1760s and 1780s. After a resounding defeat in 1792 Tipu made diplomatic overtures to France and this, combined with the threat to British India resulting from the Napoleonic invasion of Egypt, provoked the blitzkrieg of the last Mysore war. Tipu retreated into his fortified capital of Seringapatam where he made a brave last stand when the city was stormed by Colonel Baird in 1799. The destruction of the 'Tiger of Mysore' and the annexation of half his kingdom marked the opening stage in a programme of British expansion in South India. In spite of his triumph Baird was never offered an administrative post in India and eventually resigned his command because of disagreements with the Governor-General, Lord Wellesley.

Wilkie's giant canvas was commissioned as a posthumous tribute to Baird by his widow in 1838: Baird's head was adapted from an engraving after a portrait by Sir Henry Raeburn of 1814. This dramatic, Rembrandtesque painting, a monument to British heroism and a late product of the Tipu cult in Britain, was exhibited with a suitably moralising and cautionary caption: 'General Baird, who is standing in the gateway under which

Providence or poetic justice: Sir David Baird, the victor of Seringapatam, discovering the body of Tipu Sahib, the 'Tiger of Mysore', near the dungeon where he had been imprisoned for nearly four years by Tipu and his father Hyder Ali.

Tipu's Tiger

'This piece of Mechanism represents a Royal Tyger in the act of devouring a prostrate European.' This gruesome toy commissioned by Tipu Sultan, an expression of his tiger fetish and obsessive hatred of the British, was for years a prize exhibit of the East India Company after its capture at Seringapatam in 1799. 'Tipu's Tiger' is still a popular attraction at the Victoria and Albert Museum.

Tippoo received his death-wound, is supposed to be giving orders that the body should be carried to the palace; and below his feet in the parapet wall is a grating here introduced as giving light to the dungeon in which he had for nearly four years been immured by Hyder Ali and his son, the same Tippoo Sultaun, who, by a remarkable dispensation of Providence, he now finds prostrate at his feet, bereft of his crown, his kingdom, and his life.'

'This piece of Mechanism represents a Royal Tyger in the act of devouring a prostrate European. There are some barrels in imitation of an Organ, within the body of the Tyger, and a row of Keys of natural Notes. The sounds produced by the Organ are intended to resemble the Cries of a person in distress, intermixed with the roar of a Tyger. The machinery is so contrived that while the Organ is playing, the hand of the European is often lifted up, to express his helpless and deplorable condition. The whole of this design was executed by Order of Tippoo Sultaun.'

This gruesome toy was for years the prize trophy of the East India Company headquarters in London after its capture at the storming of Seringapatam in 1799. It is a cult object associated with two related obsessions – Tipu's private mythology of the tiger and hatred of the British, and British fascination with Tipu the 'sanguinary tyrant' and prototype of Oriental despotism. Tipu's tiger fetish affected almost every aspect of his daily life: one possible meaning of his name was 'tiger'; the supports of his throne were in tiger form; tiger stripes decorated the uniforms of his followers; the muzzle of his cannon were fashioned into tigers' heads and royal tigers were kept chained in front of his palace. His mechanical toy was probably a memento of an actual incident in 1792 when the only son of General Sir Hector Munro, who had routed Tipu's father in 1781, was fatally mauled by a tiger. This connection seems to be borne out by

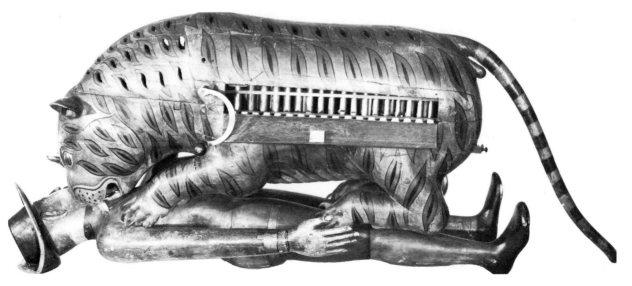

63

The Soul, a witty reminiscence of 'Tipu's Tiger' by a twentieth-century artist.

another graphic portrayal of the tragedy, – a Staffordshire pottery group of *The Death of Munrow* (sic) which bore a close resemblance to the Man-Tiger-Organ and which went on sale as a chimney ornament a few years after the toy was exhibited in London. 'Tipu's tiger' was therefore a symbol of poetic justice overtaking the British who had whittled away Tipu's dominions in successive Mysore wars.

In Britain the cult of Tipu as a favourite anti-hero took root in the 1780s and was fostered by the sensational stories relayed by his British prisoners. The near-hysterical relief which greeted the British successes against Tipu in 1792 inspired a series of paintings for the self-glorification of the victors and the exorcism of their chief bogey in South India. On the fall of Seringapatam, which coincided with the failure of Napoleon's Egyptian adventure in 1799, Tipu entered British folk history. Tipu relics were looted with official approval as presents for the royal family and unofficially as private souvenirs, and at a popular level the victory was a bonanza celebrated in paintings, prints, panoramas, stage spectacles and patriotic jingles. Over twenty-five years later the Tipu legend was still thriving when Sir Walter Scott published a minor novel called *The Surgeon's Daughter* (1827) set in the Mysore of the 1760s. Middlemas, the villain of the story, is a double agent in the service of the East India Company and also of Hyder Ali who repays his treachery by ordering him to be trampled by an elephant. Tipu appears as a conventionally lecherous Oriental from whose clutches the innocent Scottish heroine is saved by the spectacular intervention of Tipu's father Hyder Ali. The fascination of Tipu and his 'tiger' long outlasted the nineteenth century, finding belated expression in a witty primitivist painting by Jan Balet (born 1913) entitled *The Soul*.

Sir John Malcolm
1769–1833

John Malcolm, brother of Admiral Sir Pulteney Malcolm, was a younger son of George Malcolm of Burnfoot in Dumfriesshire. As the family had been impoverished by speculation, a post was sought for John with the forces of the East India Company at an exceptionally early age. He received his commission when he was only twelve and by the age of fourteen was an ensign in command of two companies of sepoys who were responsible for escorting to a place of safety the British captives released by Tipu Sahib after the second Mysore War (1780–4). At nineteen 'Boy Malcolm' decided to turn diplomat, became proficient in Persian (the diplomatic language of the East) and quitted regimental service. For the rest of his career he acted sometimes as diplomat and administrator – he played a key role in the settlement of the Mysore government after the fall of Seringapatam in 1799 – and sometimes as military commander, alternately negotiating with and campaigning against native rulers.

Although nominally a trading enterprise, the East India Company was virtually autonomous. Its concerns were not restricted to internal affairs and extended to the wider political situation of the Indian sub-continent as a whole. As early as the beginning of the nineteenth century Europe was highly sensitive to the strategic significance of Afghanistan and Persia and the desirability of dominating the approaches to India and the Indian Ocean for the furtherance of commercial and political designs. Malcolm, who made his most conspicuous contribution as an ambassador, negotiated several treaties with Indian princes on behalf of the Company and was used on successive missions to the Persian court. In 1799 he was selected as envoy to Persia – the first since the reign of Queen Elizabeth – and was instructed to induce the Shah to divert the attention of the Afghans, poised to invade the frontiers of North-West India. Two treaties were concluded: one licensed the Company to establish trading posts on the coast or in the interior of Persia, while the other bound the Shah to exclude French influence from his domains and guaranteed him naval and military support in the event of French aggression. During the administration of Lord Minto (qv) missions were despatched to Lahore, Kabul and Teheran with the aim of erecting diplomatic barriers against a potential French and Russian advance towards British India. Malcolm, who was chosen as the special envoy of the Governor-General on two occasions, stood in high favour with the Shah who wished to retain him as military adviser. The sole outcome of the mission of 1810, however, was the award of the specially created Order of the Lion and Sun of Persia to Malcolm and the introduction of potatoes into Persia by the envoy.

Malcolm's last major appointment was the governorship of the British administration in Bombay. During the intervals of his Indian service he returned to Britain in 1812 and 1822. He was a writer of some standing, an accomplished translator and the author of a *Political History of India* (1811) and a highly popular *History of Persia* (1815), and it was through his literary interests that he developed a friendship with Sir Walter Scott.

'General John Malcolm, the Persian envoy, the Delhi resident, the poet, the warrior, the polite man, and the Borderer' drawn by William Bewick on a visit to Abbotsford in 1824.

Scott first met 'General John Malcolm, the Persian envoy, the Delhi resident, the poet, the warrior, the polite man, and the Borderer' in the autumn of 1812 and renewed the acquaintance during Malcolm's second furlough. In 1824 Malcolm was again a guest at Abbotsford where William Bewick, who was visiting Scotland in the hope of bolstering his ailing finances, made a drawing of him for a gallery of distinguished contemporaries.

Henry Dundas, 1st Viscount Melville
1762–1811

Henry Dundas, son of Robert Dundas of Arniston, President of the Court of Session, entered public life as Solicitor-General in 1766. From 1774 to 1802 he was successively Member of Parliament for Midlothian and Edinburgh and in 1775 became Lord Advocate. In the 1780s he was launched on a prodigious political career as a member of the administration of William Pitt the Younger. In his capacity as government election agent Pitt's 'manager for Scotland' controlled the elections of both the Scottish representative peers and the Scottish members of the Commons and was nicknamed 'Harry the Ninth, uncrowned King of Scotland'. Pitt, whose confidence in Dundas was unbounded, loaded him with high offices including the Presidency of the Board of Control for India (1793–1801).

At the time of Dundas's appointment to the India Board Britain was vigorously asserting her ascendancy in India. The Board of Control had been set up by the India Act of 1784 to monitor the political intrigues of the East India Company and to establish the accountability of all officials in India to the British Parliament. Dundas's involvement in the administration of British India – he had been a member of the Board since its constitution – had the side effect of procuring jobs for ambitious Scots. Although individual Scots had been recorded in Company employment since the beginning of the eighteenth century, the first mass influx was attributable to his patronage which created a tradition of Scottish predominance in the Indian civil service. Sir Walter Scott, who destined his own younger son Charles for Company service, described the India Board as 'the corn chest for Scotland, where we poor gentry must send our youngest sons, as we send our black cattle to the south'. Dundas was also instrumental in securing Ceylon for Britain through his connivance in the machinations of his fellow-Scot, Hugh Cleghorn, in 1795. Cleghorn, formerly professor of Civil History at St Andrews University, engineered the defection of the mercenary troops who garrisoned Ceylon for the Dutch and seized the colony in an almost bloodless coup.

At the turn of the century Dundas's prestige in Scotland declined with the upsurge of radical agitation inspired by the French Revolution. His political career ended in 1805 when he resigned on an unproven charge of malversation and he retired to his estates to supervise the building of Melville Castle near Dalkeith.

Henry Dundas, 1st Viscount Melville, nicknamed 'Harry the Ninth, uncrowned King of Scotland', was also the influential President of the India Board which Sir Walter Scott termed 'the corn chest for Scotland where we poor gentry must send our youngest sons, as we send our black cattle to the south'.

General Sir Charles James Napier
1782–1853

One of the most unpredictable of the military Scots, Napier was the eldest son of Colonel the Honourable George Napier, a descendant of John Napier, the inventor of logarithms, and of Lady Sarah Lennox, sister of the Duke of Richmond. Having entered the army at fourteen, he was severely wounded during the Peninsular War while fighting under Sir John Moore at Corunna. Throughout the 1820s he was British political agent and administrator on the Ionian island of Cephalonia where he earned the friendship of Byron through his sympathy for the Greek nationalist cause. In the 1830s, when Australia was beginning to attract British settlement, he declined the governorship of a new colony and assumed command of the forces stationed in the north of England to quell the Chartist riots. In 1841 he was offered the chance of a lifetime – an assignment in the Indian province of Sind.

Sind was a buffer state in the North-West of India lying between the British dominions and the powerful and independent Sikh kingdom of the Punjab and was nominally subject to Afghan sovereignty. In the 1770s the East India Company had built a trading factory in the area, but the commercial potential of the Indus valley was not seriously considered until the 1830s. The instability of the Sind leadership – a confederacy of princes or 'amirs' – offered a pretext for direct intervention in 1836: a treaty of friendship provided for the temporary billeting of British troops as a deterrent to the marauding Sikhs. British fears of Russian encroachment on the North-West frontier led to the invasion of Afghanistan in 1839, ending in a debacle at Kabul. The amirs, encouraged by British discomfiture at Kabul, complained that Britain had used their territory to muster the Afghan expedition in defiance of treaty. In 1842 Napier arrived on 'the tail of the Afghan storm', bent on a military settlement of the unrest in Sind.

The 1843 campaign in Sind under the leadership of Napier was the cause of a long and heated public debate between Napier and the British Resident, Sir James Outram (qv). A disreputable piece of empire-building had been justified on the grounds of protecting the security of British India and bringing 'the blessings of civilisation' to a backward region. Napier's victory despatch read: 'Peccavi' (I have sinned). Recognising that 'We have no right to seize Sind, but . . . a very advantageous, humane piece of rascality it will be', Napier tried to make amends during his administration of the conquered province (1844–7). After serving in the first and second Sikh wars he quarrelled with the Marquess of Dalhousie (qv) over military reform and left India for good in 1851. From his departure until 1936 when it became a separate province under its own governor Sind was administered by the British authorities in Bombay. In 1947 it was assimilated into the new Dominion of Pakistan, and Karachi, which Napier had set on the road to prosperity, became the federal capital.

A formal portrait of Sir Charles James Napier,
the conqueror of Sind.

68

'Kicking up a Dust': An Alternative View of Napier

Among his contemporaries the conqueror of Sind was equally famous for his eccentricity of dress and total disregard for decorum. From *Punch* downwards his enormous pith helmet, coat of native leather and Blücher boots were the subject of innumerable jokes. The watercolour reproduced here shows Napier as remembered by his staff on the Sind campaign and corresponds to descriptions of his appearance before the battle of Miani:

> 'Napier himself rode slowly up and down between the opposing armies pouring out torrents of blasphemous exhortations so close to both sides that he was actually singed by the powder . . . His appearance was so strange that the Baluchis might well have mistaken him for a demon. Beneath a huge helmet of his own contrivance there issued a fringe of long hair at the back and in front a large pair of round spectacles, an immense hooked nose and a mane of moustache and hair reaching to his waist.'

(J W Fortescue, *History of the British Army*)

Kicking up a dust, an amateur artist's irreverent impression of Napier in action. 'His appearance was so strange that the Baluchis might well have mistaken him for a demon. Beneath a huge helmet of his own contrivance there issued a fringe of long hair at the back and in front a large pair of round spectacles, an immense hooked nose and a mane of moustache and hair reaching to his waist.'

The sketch – almost certainly done on location – is in lively contrast to the formalised and conventional public image of the military hero as presented by the bronze bust by Gamon Adams, which would have been mass-produced in small format for domestic consumption.

James Ramsay, 1st Marquess of Dalhousie
1812–1860

When he was appointed Governor-General of India, the Marquess of Dalhousie resolved: 'There can be only one master in all India, and while I am in India, I have no mind than it should be anybody else than the Governor-General in Council.'

Maharajah Duleep Singh
1838–1893

'There can only be one master in all India, and while I am in India, I have no mind than it should be anybody else than the Governor-General in Council.'

(Marquess of Dalhousie 1848)

The ablest and most energetic of Indian administrators obtained his first important government post in 1843. As head of the Railway Commission during the period when railway mania was at its height in Britain, he built up experience of railway construction and management which was to prove invaluable in India. In 1847 he arrived in India to take up office as Governor-General and was immediately drawn into the second Sikh war occasioned by the murder of two Scottish officials at Multan. The Sikh kingdom of Punjab was added to the Empire in the first of a series of controversial annexations sanctioned by Dalhousie. The fashioning of a model administration in the Punjab was personally supervised by the Governor-General. At the same time he was engaged in a demanding programme of public works and reforms providing for the extension of road, railway, canal and irrigation systems, the introduction of telegraph services, the promotion of state-aided Western education and the planning of the first three Indian universities.

The vigorous growth of British India continued with the occupation of Lower Burma on the conclusion of the second Burmese War in 1853. Further annexations were justified on the grounds of misgovernment (Oudh 1856) or by the 'doctrine of lapse' (Nagpur and Jhansi). According to this doctrine – which was already current but was used to greatest effect by Dalhousie – the states of Hindu princes without direct heirs could be taken over by the East India Company regardless of the Hindu practice of adoption. The westernising and expansionist policies of Dalhousie were later held responsible for the outbreak of the Indian Mutiny which occurred within a year of his departure.

The commanding presence of Dalhousie as Governor-General (1847–56) can be sensed in the small oil study by Sir John Watson Gordon which is related to a full-length portrait of the Marquess seated on the chair of state in the chamber of the Legislative Council which he established in 1853. As the portrait of a man invested with supreme authority it is a calculated understatement, probably containing allusions to a certain type of papal portraiture – perhaps Raphael's *Julius II* or Velasquez's *Innocent X*.

In 1838 the baby Duleep Singh, last of four 'acknowledged sons' of the reigning Maharajah Runjit Singh, was proclaimed heir to the throne of the Sikh Punjab. Runjit Singh, while successfully avoiding a debilitating collision with Britain's superior military strength, had welded his disunited country into a powerful state boasting a highly trained army on Western lines with European officers. His death in 1839 plunged the Punjab into civil strife which ended in the creation of a 'sponsored

Maharajah Duleep Singh, deposed ruler of the Sikh Punjab, erstwhile owner of the Koh-i-noor diamond, protégé of Queen Victoria and Norfolk squire.

state' under British direction. Outright annexation could not yet be countenanced and Britain was bound by treaty to protect the throne of Duleep Singh. The onset of the second Sikh war in 1848 was the signal for total annexation: the East India Company had commercial designs on the Sikh kingdom and further unrest in a territory bordering the North-West frontier could not be tolerated. Duleep, whom the British had acknowledged as rightful monarch, was deposed and stripped of his treasures, including India's most revered symbol of power, the Koh-i-noor diamond or 'mountain of light' which was now presented to Queen Victoria with the compliments of the East India Company.

In 1854 the young Maharajah left for England as the special protégé of the Queen. His popularity in London society was enhanced by his recent conversion to Christianity. Dalhousie, who had taken great pains to assure the Sikhs that no undue pressure had been exerted in proselytizing their prince, felt his conscience eased: 'I have never from the hour in which I signed the decree had one moment's hesitation or doubt as to the justice or necessity of my act in dethroning the boy. If I had such a doubt, the sight of the blessed result for him, to which that act has led, would now have thoroughly consoled me . . .' Moreover: 'Politically we could desire nothing better, for it destroys his possible influence for ever.' Duleep the aspiring European was frequently photographed and painted, often at the royal command. As Dalhousie commented approvingly in 1854: 'The "night-cappy" appearance of his turban is his strongest national feature. Do away with that and he has no longer any outward and visible sign of a Sikh about him'. During the early years of his exile the Maharajah was a favourite guest of the royal family and became a keen if mediocre photographer under the personal tuition of the Prince Consort. A shared enthusiasm for photography and field sports brought him the lifelong friendship of Ronald Leslie Melville, heir to the Earl of Leven. By way of completing his accession to the landed gentry Duleep rented a succession of shooting estates in Scotland before acquiring his own property of Elveden in Norfolk as a rival attraction to the Prince of Wales's establishment at Sandringham.

Queen Victoria's favour remained constant although her Maharajah rejected the royal choice of a bride and married an illegitimate half-European convert from a Cairo mission school. Trouble developed in the 1860s when he complained of the inadequacy of his government pension and, infuriated by the prevarication of the India Office, reasserted his claim to the Sikh throne, conducting an hysterical campaign in the Press and even making a personal visit to Russia in a vain attempt to enlist anti-British support. From his retreat in Paris he continued to advertise himself as 'England's implacable foe' but by the 1890s, having auctioned most of his jewels, he was forced to capitulate and seek reconciliation with the government with the help of the still tolerant Queen Victoria. He died an impoverished maverick and a pathetic relic of the British Raj.

Colonel Alexander Gardner
(about 1801–1877)

As a mercenary of Kashmir, the Scottish-American (or perhaps Irish) adventurer Alexander Gardner presented 'a most peculiar and striking appearance, clothed from head to foot in the 79th tartan, but fashioned by a native tailor. Even his pagri was of tartan, and it was adorned with the egret's plume, only allowed to persons of high rank.'

'Gardiner's life history . . . well deserves the attention of our rising manhood in the British Isles. Though not relating to the British dominions, or the British service itself, it shows what men of British race can do under stress of trial and suffering. It illustrates the self-contained spirit of adventure in individuals which has done so much towards the founding of the British Empire, and may yet help in extending the empire to all quarters of the globe.'

(Sir Richard Temple)

In the estimation of his admiring contemporaries Alexander Gardner was the Scottish soldier of fortune *par excellence* and a shining example to the British Raj. According to his own account he was born in the 1780s, the son of a Scottish emigrant who fought in the American War of Independence, and left Canada in 1812 to join his brother who was working as an engineer in Astrakhan. On the death of his brother he decided to seek his fortune in Persia and spent several years roving around Central Asia, travelling with native caravans. In 1823 he made his way to Kabul, finding employment with Habibulla Khan, the dispossessed nephew of Dost Mohammed Khan who was the effective ruler of northern and eastern Afghanistan. As a reward for his services Gardner was given one of the royal attendants in marriage. In 1826 Habibulla Khan was finally defeated by his uncle and in the course of the fighting Gardner's Afghan wife and child were killed.

Gardner allegedly left Afghanistan in 1831 and became commander of artillery to Runjit Singh, ruler of the Punjab which is now part of West Pakistan. He was one of a number of foreign officers recruited by Runjit Singh for the purpose of building up a European-style army to counter the threat of a British or an Afghan invasion. Prior to the consolidation of British rule internecine strife was a recurrent hazard of life in India and it was primarily for this reason and not for that of a prospective conflict with the British that Indian rulers maintained private armies. The successes of sepoys in the armies of Lawrence, Clive and the eighteenth-century French commanders against untrained Indian troops of vastly superior numbers had convinced native rulers of the advisability of employing European officers. In consequence India became a mecca for adventurers of all nationalities with a forceful personality and some military experience. The security and status of foreign mercenaries in the Punjab were entirely dependent on the whim of Runjit Singh and the regular agreements to which they were bound might be unilaterally disregarded. Under the terms of their service they were enjoined to 'domesticate themselves in the country by marriage, not to eat beef, nor smoke tobacco in public, to permit their beards to grow, to take care not to offend against the Sikh religion, and if required, to fight against their own country'. Control of the highly-prized artillery was jealously guarded by the Maharajah and the power of his European subordinates, mostly deserters from the East India Company forces, was strictly monitored. In 1839 the death of Runjit Singh plunged the newly united country into a prolonged civil war. Eventually the succession passed to the last survivor of his line, the boy Duleep Singh, whose state was later annexed for Britain by the Marquess of Dalhousie.

In his last years Gardner is said to have served as artillery commander to the Maharajah of Kashmir under British protection. One of Gardner's many visitors in Kashmir left a description of him in old age: ' . . . a most peculiar and striking appearance, clothed from head to foot in the 79th tartan (the 79th Cameron Highlanders who were based in India), but fashioned by a native tailor. Even his pagri was of tartan, and it was adorned with the egret's plume, only allowed to persons of high rank. I imagine he lived entirely in native fashion: he was said to be wealthy, and the owner of many villages'.

Gardner's venerable age, which he increased by some twenty years, undoubtedly contributed to the credibility of the persona which he presented to would-be biographers. The scanty documentation contained in official records would still have been sufficient to invalidate practically all the early chapters of his story: his alter ego was probably an Irishman from Clongoose and an ordinary deserter from the British army or navy with a lively imagination and few scruples about appropriating the experiences of others for his own glorification. While he readily admitted having witnessed some of the outrages committed during the anarchy in the Punjab, he did not disclose that he owed his promotion to the mutilation of a prisoner, an atrocity which the Hindus present refused to carry out. As for his assumed nationality, Scottish-American ancestry evidently held an aura of romance which was calculated to captivate his listeners: 'To take the two ends of the long tangled line is something wonderful. The one bright and sunny, on the banks of Lake Superior in the Far West; the other approaching where the chapter will close, on the banks of the Indus . . . Faithful to his standard, whatever that might have been . . . he presented, and perhaps still presents, one of the finest specimens ever known of the soldier of fortune' (Sir Henry Durand).

INDIAN MISSION

'And would you keep your spiritual sympathies pent up within the craggy ramparts of the Grampians? . . . Let us awake, arise, and rescue unhappy India from its present and impending horrors . . . Let us arise and revive the genius of olden time: let us revive the spirit of our forefathers . . . Like them let us enter into a Solemn League and Covenant before our God, on behalf of that benighted land, that we will not rest, till the voice of praise and thanksgiving arise, in daily orisons, from its coral strands, roll over its fertile plains, resound from its smiling valleys, and re-echo from its everlasting hills.'

(Alexander Duff 1835)

In the nineteenth century India was second only to Africa as a field for Scottish missions. The upsurge of intensive European evangelism coincided with the building of the British Empire in India. The impetus was provided by the founder of the Baptist Missionary Society, William Carey, who settled in Calcutta in 1793. From the start he was opposed by the all-powerful East India Company which feared that missionary propaganda might precipitate social and political discontent and so militate against its own interests. Not until 1833 were missionaries allowed complete freedom of movement within Company territory. Representatives of the London Missionary Society, the Society for the Propagation of Christian Knowledge and the Church of England Missionary Society followed Carey and in 1822 the Scottish Missionary Society penetrated western India.

In 1824 the General Assembly of the Church of Scotland voted in favour of foreign missions, its first objective being India. The arrival of John Wilson (1829) and the Church of Scotland pioneer Alexander Duff (1830) opened a new era. They were the advance guard of a new type of missionary, sophisticated, highly educated and sharing the characteristically Scottish enthusiasm for education. Duff set out from the conviction that it was time to present the Gospel to the intellectual elite of India with the ultimate aim of educating and converting the whole population. The development of the mission school system between 1830 and the Indian Mutiny was largely due to his initiative which strongly influenced government policy on Indian education. Duff was also an eloquent publicist whose impassioned address to the General Assembly of 1835 did much to augment Scottish support for missions to India.

The Mutiny of 1857 quickened Britain's consciousness of the crucial importance of her Indian Empire to her status as a world power and induced a new sense of moral responsibility towards India. The results were seen in the proliferation of English and Scottish missions and their concentration in the northern provinces affected by the rebellion.

Reverend Alexander Duff
1806–1878

In 1824 the Church of Scotland, which had just approved a forward policy of overseas mission, received a petition from the East India Company chaplain in Calcutta. In response it issued an open letter to the people of Scotland on the national duty of mission and in 1829 Alexander Duff from Moulin in Perthshire, a brilliant student at St Andrews University, was ordained in St George's, Edinburgh (now West Register House), as pioneer missionary to India. Duff's impact on Indian mission was to be more decisive than that of any other individual.

By 1830 missionaries were already operating in Calcutta and Bengal, but with scant success. With the exception of William Carey at Serampore, they relied on wayside preaching and elementary tuition carried out in the native languages. Most of their converts were lower caste and made little impression on the Hindus. In direct opposition to public and missionary opinion Duff embarked on a revolutionary project to transform Hindu society from the highest level: 'We shall, with the blessing

Reverend Alexander Duff, the most influential Scottish missionary to India.

of God, devote our time and strength to the preparing of a mine, and the setting of a train which shall one day explode and tear up the whole from the lowest depth.' His early work was undertaken in cooperation with the great Indian reformer Rammohan Roy who offered Duff the premises for a school and recruited his first Hindu pupils. His method was the adoption of English as the language of teaching, of Christian propaganda and of the 'civilising' process in general. Within a week his school had three hundred applicants. Missionaries in Bombay, Madras and Nagpur followed his lead in evolving a mission school system and within five years government policy on Indian education reflected Duff's thinking. His plans were supported by Lord William Bentinck, the Governor-General of the time, who shared his confidence in education as 'the panacea for the regeneration of India'. Duff's influence shaped the famous despatch of 1854 from Lord Halifax, President of the Board of Control, to the Marquess of Dalhousie. This advocated the establishment of universities at Calcutta, Bombay and Madras modelled on the University of London and the inauguration of a system of government grants-in-aid to schools and laid down the pattern of education in India for the next century.

As a consequence of his secession to the Free Church Duff had to surrender the mission property and premises in Calcutta in 1843. Such was his prestige among Anglo-Indian Christians that the financial security of the Calcutta mission was scarcely jeopardised by the Disruption of the Church of Scotland and a rural station at Bansberia was endowed with the prize-money or 'blood money' awarded to Sir James Outram for his part in the conquest of Sind. In 1850 Duff visited Scotland for a second time to canvass further support for Indian mission and, at the unusually early age of forty-five, was elected Moderator of the Free Church Assembly. Following a much publicised tour of the United States in 1854 he returned to India in 1856 to superintend the constitution of the new University of Calcutta. Ill-health finally obliged Duff to leave India in 1863. On his way home he toured the Free Church stations in South Africa, initiating a reform of educational policy at Lovedale. Back in Edinburgh he became the first missionary professor at New College and, as convener of the Foreign Missions Committee of the Free Church, supervised the implementation of Livingstone's scheme for a Scottish mission to Nyasaland.

Reverend John Wilson
1804–1875

John Wilson, the most influential Scottish missionary in India after Alexander Duff, was the son of a burgh councillor of Lauder in Berwickshire. His attention was initially drawn to India when he was tutor to the sons of Sir John Rose, a Scottish soldier in India. After studying theology and medicine at the University of Edinburgh he approached the Scottish Missionary Society, a non-denominational association founded in 1796, which had recently begun work in Western India.

On arrival in Bombay Mrs Wilson, who had studied at Aberdeen University and was a remarkably well-educated

woman for her time, opened the first school for girls in Western India in 1829. The following year Alexander Duff reached India and Wilson, stimulated by the extraordinary success of his educational programme, became in Bombay the equivalent of Duff in Calcutta. Primary schools were supplemented by the foundation of a higher English school. In contrast to Duff, Wilson placed more emphasis on female education and teaching in the vernacular, but his results were no less controversial and the conversion of two of his pupils involved him in legal proceedings with the Parsi community (see Dhanjibhai Nauroji).

In 1842 Wilson returned to Scotland on his first furlough and took the opportunity for a pilgrimage to the Holy Land which he later described in his *Lands of the Bible* published in 1847. It was during this visit to Scotland that he was photographed by D O Hill and Robert Adamson. Wilson may have chosen to have himself portrayed in Palestinian dress as a discreet form of publicity for his forthcoming publication. More probably the costume simply appealed to the calotypists as a subject for 'artistic' photography. During his travels he had received news of the Disruption and, like all the overseas missionaries of the Established Church, declared his allegiance to the new Free Church. The immediate effects of the Disruption on the Indian missions were devastating. Wilson was compelled to give up his high school – a loss which was not made good until 1855. Notwithstanding, he continued to expand the horizons of the Bombay mission and in 1849 toured the newly conquered province of Sind with Alexander Duff.

During the Indian Mutiny Wilson's talents as a linguist made him indispensable to the British administration, for whom he deciphered the rebels' secret despatches. In the year of the Mutiny he was appointed dean of the faculty of arts and examiner in Oriental languages at the University of Bombay. On his recall to Scotland as the second missionary Moderator of the Free Church in 1870, the citizens of Bombay endowed a lectureship in philology in his honour. He died near Bombay in 1875.

Reverend Dhanjibhai Nauroji
1822–1908

Soon after the inauguration of the Missionary Institute in Bombay a Parsi boy called Dhanjibhai Nauroji was enrolled as a pupil of the Reverend John Wilson. The Parsis, a people originating in the city of Pars or Persis, were followers of the Zoroastrian religion. Dhanjibhai's conversion to Christianity and baptism in 1839 caused a furore among the Parsi community in Bombay. Having failed to storm the mission house, they began legal proceedings against Wilson, claiming that the proselyte was being held against his will. Although Wilson won the case the majority of his Parsi pupils were promptly withdrawn from the school by their outraged parents.

In 1842 Dhanjibhai, who had been accepted for the ministry, accompanied Wilson to Scotland, travelling by way of Egypt, Arabia and the Holy Land. The following year he entered New College and in 1846 was ordained missionary by Dr Candlish in Canonmills Hall, Edinburgh, before a huge assembly. From

The conversion of Wilson's Parsi pupil Dhanjibhai Nauroji caused a furore in Bombay. He accompanied his teacher to Palestine and then to Scotland and followed Wilson's example in adhering to the newly formed Free Church.

1847 until his death at the age of eighty-six Wilson's first Parsi convert worked in the Bombay Presidency as a missionary and a recognised leader of the Indian Church.

The calotype photograph of Dhanjibhai with the Reverend John Jaffray, like most portraits of clergy taken by Hill and Adamson, was a study for Hill's Disruption Picture, a huge painting representing the Signing of the Deed of Demission which resulted in the breakaway formation of the Free Church in May 1843. Hill, who witnessed the schism, was so moved that he decided to record the occasion – a project which presented the formidable problem of having to execute portraits of all the delegates before they dispersed to all parts of Scotland. The eminent physicist Sir David Brewster, who had brought Fox Talbot's calotype process to Scotland and had experimented with it in St Andrews in collaboration with the chemist Dr John Adamson, heard of Hill's intentions and proposed that he should use calotypes as a substitute for preliminary sketches. Brewster accordingly introduced Hill to John Adamson's younger brother, Robert, with whom he went into partnership. Over the next four years Hill and Adamson took photographs of the majority of the delegates and of other Free Church ministers who had not actually attended the assembly. Among these was

Dhanjibhai Nauroji who had been entering Jerusalem with Wilson on the day of the Disruption. The Disruption Picture itself was not completed until 1866.

Reverend Stephen Hislop
1817–1863

Reverend Stephen Hislop, anthropologist and missionary, was drawn to Central India by the combined influence of Duff and Wilson.

In 1842 an Army officer's wife who was stricken with cholera in Jalna made a dying request to her husband to use all her money for the foundation of a Christian mission in the province of Nagpur. With the support of the Reverend John Wilson of Bombay the newly formed Free Church of Scotland ordained Stephen Hislop of Duns in Berwickshire as leader of the mission.

Hislop was drawn to India by the combined influence of Duff and Wilson and was closely guided by their principles. In his memorial recommending the project Wilson had stressed the strategic position of Nagpur as a route centre attracting travellers from all parts of the sub-continent: several of Hislop's converts were soldiers who contributed to his success by spreading the Gospel further afield. Hislop, an outspoken critic of both native rulers and British officials, was a gifted linguist and anthropologist who pioneered research on the language and culture of the Gonds in accordance with Wilson's practice of studying local customs and religious beliefs and mastering the vernacular. The difficulties of village evangelism in India caused by the so-called 'brutish ignorance' of the people made education his first priority. His schools, based on those of Duff and Wilson, were so highly regarded that in the 1860s the British Government was excused the need to establish a college of higher education in Nagpur at official expense. Female education – a controversial issued in nineteenth-century India – was introduced into Nagpur by Hislop's wife. Having narrowly survived the Indian Mutiny, Hislop was drowned in 1863 while crossing a flooded stream.

THE INDIAN MUTINY 1857

'Here we had not only a servile war and a sort of Jacquerie combined, but we had a war of religion, a war of race, and a war of revenge, of hope, of some national promptings to shake off the yoke of a stranger, and to re-establish the full power of native chiefs, and the full sway of native religions.'

(William Howard Russell of *The Times* 1858)

'Oh, East is East, and West is West, and never the twain shall meet'

(Rudyard Kipling)

The British occupation of India lasted just under two centuries. During the first century when Britain 'conquered and peopled half the world in a fit of absence of mind' the East India Company extended its influence over three-fifths of the Indian sub-continent. By 1857 Anglo-Indian confidence was at a premium, reflecting Palmerston's belief that 'we stand at the head of moral, social and political civilisation'. Among Indians of every class, however, there was profound unease and disaffection. British attempts to consolidate power by imposing a rational and efficient administration implied a transformation of traditional Indian society. Princes and landowners felt threatened with extinction as a consequence of Dalhousie's 'doctrine of lapse'. In the eighteenth century the East India Company had had a vested interest in maintaining the *status quo*. As the administration became progressively more anglicised officials developed a sense of racial, cultural and spiritual superiority, carrying out reforms with scant regard for customary laws or religious practices. A reaction to the indiscriminate modernizing and crusading zeal of the British became inevitable.

Discontent exploded into open rebellion in the centenary year of Clive's victory at Plassey. Its immediate cause was the introduction into the Bengal Army of Enfield rifles supplied with cartridges greased with cows' and pigs' fat, unclean to both Hindus and Moslems. This supposedly confirmed suspicions of a British conspiracy to subvert traditional religions and break caste – suspicions which had been aggravated by the unprecedented spread of missionary activity. In 1857 violence erupted in the North-West Provinces which were already seething with resentment over the annexation of Oudh in the previous year: three regiments at Meerut shot their officers and marched on Delhi. Although the military revolt was mainly confined to the Bengal Army dispossessed rulers also grasped this opportunity for revenge. The British, caught off guard with their forces depleted by the recent Crimean War, took fourteen months of bitter fighting to crush the Mutiny, aided by the disintegration of the rebel leadership. Most of the senior commands were entrusted to Scots – Colin Campbell, James Outram, James Hope Grant and Hugh Rose – who became heroes of the legends surrounding the famous sieges of Cawnpore/Kanpur and Lucknow.

Outline of Events		
	March 1857	Unrest among Bengal regiments over greased cartridges
	May 1857	Outbreak of rebellion at Meerut; seizure of Delhi; mutiny at Lucknow
	June 1857	Mutiny at Cawnpore; massacre of the evacuating British garrison
	July 1857	Siege of British Residency in Lucknow; massacre of British women and children captured at Cawnpore ordered by Nana Sahib; Cawnpore retaken by British the following day
	September 1857	First 'relief'/reinforcement of Lucknow by Havelock and Outram; Delhi recaptured by British
	November 1857	Second relief of Lucknow by Sir Colin Campbell

March 1858– May 1859	'Clearing up' operations in Central India led by Sir Colin Campbell and Major-General Rose
November 1858	Royal Proclamation abolishes East India Company India placed under direct rule of British Government

INCIDENTS DURING THE MUTINY
The Second Relief of Lucknow

An artist's reconstruction of the reunion of the British commanders after the second relief of Lucknow in the autumn of 1857.

The reunion of the British commanders in November 1857 after the second relief of Lucknow effected by Sir Colin Campbell was commemorated in a famous painting by Thomas Jones Barker. Barker specialised in panoramic representations of recent historical events of which the best-known was a study of the allied generals in conference before Sebastopol in the Crimea, adapted from photographs by the pioneer war photographer Roger Fenton. His reconstruction of the occasion at Lucknow was executed in 1859 from sketches taken on the spot by Egron Lundgren and was reproduced in the form of large engravings to cater for popular demand. Among the most prominent figures are Sir Henry Havelock who is shown shaking hands with Sir Colin Campbell, Sir James Outram, Sir James Hope Grant (on horseback), Sir William Mansfield (Campbell's chief-of-staff) and Sir Rober Napier, later Lord Napier of Magdala.

Cawnpore after the Massacre

The Indian Mutiny produced a high quota of horror stories, some of which were relayed in the graphic revelations of William Howard Russell, the special correspondent of *The Times*.

Sir Colin Campbell's troops photographed by Felice Beato among the ruins of Cawnpore, site of the notorious massacre of the British garrison and their wives and children.

Tensions on both sides were extreme and were reflected in the savagery of the fighting. The inflation of some incidents into legends was some measure of the shock registered in mid-Victorian Britain and the lasting disenchantment caused by this violent rejection of the British version of Western Christian civilisation.

In this photograph by Felice Beato (a gifted amateur photographer who had made his debut in the Crimea and was commissioned by the War Office to take documentary photographs in India) some of Sir Colin Campbell's troops are posing among the ruins of Cawnpore, the site of one of the most notorious episodes of the Mutiny. When Cawnpore was seized by the rebels in the summer of 1857 Nana Sahib, in breach of safe-conduct, ordered the successive massacres of the British garrison and their wives and children. The British troops who re-captured Cawnpore repaid atrocity with atrocity and further vengeance was exacted after the relief of Lucknow in the autumn. The following extract is taken from one of the less lurid eye-witness accounts of the scene at Cawnpore and was written by Sergeant William Forbes-Mitchell of Sir Colin Campbell's 93rd Sutherland Highlanders:

'We then went to see the slaughter-house in which the un-fortunate women and children had been barbarously murdered; and the well into which the mangled bodies were afterwards flung . . . It was long before our feelings could be controlled. The floors of the rooms were still covered with congealed blood, littered with trampled, torn dresses of women and children, shoes, slippers, and locks of long hair, many of which had evidently been severed from the living scalps by sword-cuts. But among the traces of barbarous torture and cruelty which excited horror and a desire for revenge, one stood out prominently beyond all others. It was an iron hook fixed into the wall of one of the rooms in the house, about six feet from the floor . . . This hook was covered with dried blood, and from the marks on the whitewashed wall, it was evident that a little child had been hung on it by the neck with its face to the wall . . . The number of victims butchered in the house, counted and buried in the well by General Havelock's force, was one hundred and eighteen women and ninety-two children.

Up to the date of my visit, a brigade-order, issued by Brigadier-General J G S Neill, First Madras Fusiliers, was still in force . . . Its purport was to this effect: That, after trial and condemnation, all the prisoners found guilty of having taken part in the murder of European women and children were to be taken into the slaughter-house by Major Bruce's mehtar police [sweepers – the lowest caste of all] and there made to crouch down, and with their mouths lick clean a square foot of the blood-stained floor before being taken out to the gallows and hanged . . . It remained in force till the arrival of Sir Colin Campbell in Cawnpore on the 3rd November 1857, when he promptly put a stop to it as unworthy of the English name and a Christian Government.'

Sir James Hope Grant
1808–1875

James Hope Grant was a younger son of a Perthshire family, the Grants of Kilgraston, whose wealth derived from estates in Scotland and Jamaica. He entered the army as a cornet in the 9th Lancers to start a brilliant career as both a regimental and a general officer, serving in most of the major campaigns in China and India.

In China he saw action in the 'Opium War' of 1839–42 when Hongkong became a British possession. Again in 1860, with Charles George Gordon as his subordinate (qv), he led the British contingent of the combined Franco-British force which was endeavouring to 'encourage' the Emperor of China to honour trading treaties imposed on him by the European powers. It was, however, in India that Hope Grant particularly distinguished himself. As a regimental officer he took part in the two campaigns against the Sikhs which led to the annexation of the Punjab in 1849. During the Mutiny he served at the siege of, and assault on, Delhi, at Lucknow and Cawnpore, and commanded flying columns during the concluding operations in Oudh. After the second China campaign Grant returned to India to assume command of the Madras Army. His career ended in Britain where he was deployed as an able military administrator and theorist from 1865.

This handsome but conventional military portrait by the sitter's younger brother Francis, the fashionable society portrait painter, was probably worked up from sketches taken in 1851 while Grant was in Britain on sick leave. Hope Grant is wearing the full dress uniform of a Lieutenant-Colonel of the 9th Lancers, his regiment from 1826 to 1858. The artist, who had no direct experience of India, has tried to suggest an Oriental setting by

General Sir James Hope Grant: a stylish portrait with an 'Indian' setting by his brother, the society portrait painter, Sir Francis Grant.

introducing a few palm trees into the background. Sir Francis painted several other portraits of his brother as military hero and in the less predictable role of musician. Hope Grant was a talented amateur 'cellist who was regularly accompanied on campaigns by an enormous violincello, carried on a camel. Natives ran away from it whenever it appeared, calling it . . . "the devil".'

Sir James Outram
1803–1863

Like many of the military Scots in India Outram was the younger son of an impecunious landed family. At sixteen he sailed for India as an infantry cadet in the Bombay Army. His

84

'The Bayard of India' shortly before his death in 1863. Sir Joseph Fayrer noted in his diary: 'On the 28th of March I received, to my great sorrow, a telegram that my dear old friend Sir James Outram had died at Paris on March the 12th . . . He had quite recently, at my request, allowed my friend Mr Alfred Buxton to paint his portrait in Paris, and the likeness is good, but he looks so emaciated and worn as scarcely to be recognisable as my vigorous and robust friend of former days.'

contemporary reputation rested on his dual role as political agent and military commander in the 1843 campaign in Sind and during the Indian Mutiny. As British Resident (political representative at a native court) in the troubled province of Sind on the Afghan border he won the trust and cooperation of the Amir, a faithful if unwilling ally of the British. In 1842 Outram returned from campaigning in the first Afghan war to find that the unrest in Sind was about to be settled by military intervention. At first Sir Charles Napier, the British commander in Sind, was full of praise for Outram whom he christened 'the Bayard of India' after the gallant captain of François I. Napier, however, had instructions from the Governor-General Lord Ellenborough to annex the province. A swift campaign added Sind to the Empire and sparked off a public quarrel between Napier and Outram who vigorously condemned the Government's aggressive action.

In 1854 Outram was appointed by Dalhousie to the Residency of Oudh which was soon to become a core area of the Mutiny. The following year he reluctantly recommended annexation as the only practicable remedy for native 'misgovernment' of the province. The annexation of Oudh worsened an already explosive situation. Within a year Outram found himself in action against the mutineers with Colonel Robert Napier, the future Lord Napier of Magdala. With Henry Havelock, Outram led the first abortive assault on Lucknow, only to discover that he had simply reinforced the beleaguered garrison and was himself effectively besieged until he was relieved by the Commander-in-Chief, Sir Colin Campbell. During 'clearing up' operations in Oudh he was joined by Sir James Hope Grant in charge of the cavalry. For the remainder of his time in India Outram served as military adviser to the Governor-General in Council and was instrumental in promoting the reorganisation of the Indian Army. In 1858 he was created a baronet and finally retired from India in 1860.

Alfred Buxton's sombre portrait of Outram in a sad state of decline was commissioned in Paris shortly before Outram's death by his friend and colleague, the distinguished physician Sir Joseph Fayrer. After the annexation of Oudh – the last major act of Dalhousie's administration – Outram had been named Chief Commissioner of the new British dependency and Fayrer had been appointed Civil Surgeon of Lucknow, remaining in India throughout the Mutiny. An amusing impression of Outram as Fayrer would have remembered him in 1857 was sketched by a young officer on Outram's staff: 'When I called on him one day I found him in his shirt sleeves and a pair of old military pantaloons sitting on his bed smoking a cheroot. He was not by any means a handsome man, broad and powerful looking with frizzly dark hair . . . I had hardly seated myself when he offered me a cigar which I thankfully accepted, they are scarce enough in camp . . . The General never ceased smoking and he was most liberal with them. He also gave dinner parties daily to which we were all asked in turn.'

Sir Colin Campbell, Lord Clyde
1792–1863

Colin MacIver, the son of a Glasgow carpenter, assumed his mother's maiden name when he entered the army as an ensign in 1807. This was the height of the Napoleonic wars and he remained on almost constant active service until 1813 when he was invalided out of the army because of wounds. Having re-enlisted in 1816, he slowly advanced in rank until in 1841 he was promoted to command a battalion in the 'Opium War' in China. In the late 1840s he distinguished himself in the campaign against the Sikhs in the Punjab and on the North-West frontier in what is now Pakistan.

Campbell's subsequent reputation rests on campaigns conducted when he was already in his sixties. During the Crimean War of 1854 Campbell was brigade commander of the Highland Brigade of the First Division which included the 93rd Highlanders. Under his leadership the 93rd turned the tide against the Russians at the battle of the Alma and repulsed the onslaught of the Cossacks on their 'thin red streak tipped with a line of steel' at Balaclava. The episode of the 'Thin Red Line' at Balaclava – in the famous catchphrase coined by William Howard Russell of *The Times* – earned Campbell a lasting

accolade as a popular hero. Something of the atmosphere of that fierce encounter and its extraordinary conclusion in the Charge of the Light Brigade is captured in a letter from Colonel Alexander Leith Hay, written two days after the event:

'The day before yesterday we had a tremendous fight. We were the only English Regt. here with the exception of Cavalry and Artillery – only two troops of the latter – but we had in Army redoubts on our front, 4 in number, about 3000 Turks, 3 or 4000 more with us in position. At daybreak the enemy attacked our position in large force, about 20,000 men, and in two hours had taken 3 out of 4 of our advanced posts from our faithful allies. They then sent down upon us 4 columns of infantry and a cloud of cavalry but were afraid to advance their guns so near our batteries. The infantry halted just out of range of our rifles, and down came a cloud of regular cavalry, about 2000 on our devoted heads. The Turks broke and fled to a man. We with old Sir Colin Campbell at our head received them in line of 4 deep, waited till their leading squadrons came to within 40 yards and then delivered such a fire into them as I think has seldom been equalled . . . emptying about 150 saddles at the first volley. They turned and fled in great disorder . . . and retired to beyond the heights . . . Our cavalry by this time came up. Dozens of magnificent charges took place entirely in our form although our force was much outnumbered, say 10 to 1, and everything went well until the Light Brigade of Cavalry under Ld. Cardigan must needs attempt to take two heavy batteries of field guns, not seeing that large bodies of the enemies' horse masked others on the flanks. They went at it in fine style, but had no sooner taken the guns than the enemy opened out and the cavalry charged. The result of this mad act was that out of 800 sabres which went into action only 250 mustered on parade. The enemy retired out of sight and so ended the battle of Balaclava.'

(Letter from Colonel Alexander Leith Hay to his mother, 27 October 1854: Leith Hay Muniments, the National Trust for Scotland, deposited in the Scottish Record Office)

Sir Colin Campbell as Commander-in-Chief during the Mutiny with his friend and chief-of-staff, Sir William Mansfield, in a photograph taken by Felice Beato. *The Times* reporter, William Howard Russell, observed: 'Sir Colin in spite of a slight stoop, is every inch a soldier in look and bearing – spare, muscular, well poised on small, well-made feet . . . His figure shows little trace of fifty years of the hardest and most varied service . . . General Mansfield, taller than his chief, well-made and broad-chested, gives some indications of his extra-ordinary labours of the desk and study in a 'scholar's slope' about the shoulders . . .'

On the strength of his Crimean reputation Campbell was given supreme command of the British forces in India and was generally credited with the swift suppression of the Mutiny. Among his subordinates his thoroughness and caution had been rewarded with the nickname of 'Sir Crawling Camel' and his critics thought him 'too cautious for India'. By the time he reached India Delhi had been re-captured and Cawnpore re-covered. Campbell organised an all-European army which he led in the second and final relief of Lucknow and was able to evacuate the civilian population successfully. Over the next ten months he re-established British authority in Northern India by a series of well planned operations and much hard fighting. He returned to Britain to be showered with honours and raised to the peerage.

AFTERMATH: THE END OF 'JOHN COMPANY'

The suppression of the Mutiny marked the advent of a new India, 'the breakdown of the old system and the renunciation of the attempt to effect an impossible compromise between the Asiatic and European view of things, legal, military and administrative' (Fitzjames Stephen). The rebel leadership were distinguished by their lack of any real community of aims and in military terms the revolt was a comparatively small-scale affair, but the shock registered in mid-Victorian Britain was profound and the Mutiny mentality of distrust and cultural conflict lingered on. Indirect government through the intermediary of the East India Company gave way to direct Crown rule, fortified by a restructured Indian Army. As the figurehead of the new régime, Queen Victoria took her responsibilities very seriously and by the time of her proclamation as Empress of India in 1877 had convinced the majority of her Indian subjects of her personal dedication to their welfare.

FURTHER READING

General
Andrew Dewar Gibb, *Scottish Empire* (London 1937)
Gordon Donaldson, *The Scots Overseas* (London 1966)
R Hyams, *Britain's Imperial Century 1815–1914* (London 1976)

North America
George Pratt Insh, *Scottish Colonial Schemes* (Glasgow 1922)
Nellis M Crouse, *The Search for the North-West Passage* (New York 1934)
A Basil Lubbock, *The Arctic Whalers* (Glasgow 1937)
W S Shepperson, *British Emigration to North America* (Oxford 1957)
E E Rich, *The History of the Hudson's Bay Company 1670–1870* vol I (London 1958)
Ernest S Dodge, *Northwest by Sea* (New York 1961)
Leslie H Neatby, *The Search for Franklin* (London 1970)
Douglas Hill, *The Scots to Canada* (London 1972)
George Malcolm Thomson, *The North-West Passage* (London 1975)
Alan Cooke and Clive Holland, *The Exploration of Northern Canada* (Arctic History Press 1977)

Africa
Captain Henry Hozier and Major Trevenen J Holland, *Record of the Expedition to Abyssinia* 2 vols (London 1870)
Robert Hunter, *History of the Foreign Missions of the Free Church of Scotland in India and Africa* (London 1873)
J Duplessis, *A History of the Christian Missions in South Africa* (London 1911)
Roland Oliver, *The Missionary Factor in East Africa* (London 1952)
H C Thompson, *The Kuruman Mission* (Kuruman 1952)
Jack Simmons, *Livingstone and Africa* (London 1955)
ed Margery Perham and J Simmons, *African Discovery. An Anthology of Exploration* (London 1957)
Cecil Northcott, *Christianity in Africa* (London 1963)
Charles Pelham Groves, *The Planting of Christianity in Africa* 2 vols (London 1964)
P D Curtin, *The Image of Africa. British Ideas and Actions 1780–1850* (London 1965)
Julian Symons, *England's Pride. The Story of the Gordon Relief Expedition* (London 1965)
John Marlowe, *Mission to Khartoum* (London 1969)
Frederick Myatt, *The March to Magdala* (London 1970)
Freda Troup, *South Africa. An Historical Introduction* (London 1972)
Christopher Lloyd, *The Search for the Niger* (London 1973)
M E Chamberlain, *The Scramble for Africa* (London 1974)
J D Fage and Roland Oliver, *A Short History of Africa* (Harmondsworth 1979)

India
Julius Richter, *A History of Missions in India* (London 1908)
ed H L O Garrett, C Grey, *European Adventurers of Northern India 1785 to 1849* (Lahore 1929)
ed Michael Edwardes: William Howard Russell, *My Indian Mutiny Diary* (London 1957)
Elizabeth Hewat, *Vision and Achievement 1796–1856. A History of the Foreign Missions of the Churches United in the Church of Scotland* (London 1960)
ed Michael Edwardes: William Forbes-Mitchell, *The Relief of Lucknow* (London 1962)
H Furber, *John Company at Work* (Harvard 1965)
J A B Palmer, *The Mutiny Outbreak at Meerut in 1857* (Cambridge 1966)
ed James Hewitt, *Eye-Witnesses to the Indian Mutiny* (Reading 1972)
Percival Spear, *A History of India* vol II (Harmondsworth 1978)
Mildred Archer, *India and British Portraiture 1770–1825* (London 1979)
Christopher Hibbert, *The Great Mutiny India 1857* (Harmondsworth 1980)

Monographs and manuscript sources are not listed.

LIST OF ILLUSTRATIONS

43 Henry Morton Stanley (1841–1904). Carte-de-visite photograph by the London Stereoscopic Company, 1872: 'Mr Stanley, in the dress he wore when he met Livingstone in Africa.' *Scottish National Portrait Gallery*.

44 Reverend William Govan (1804–1875). Calotype photograph by D O Hill and Robert Adamson; study for the Disruption Picture, about 1846. *Scottish National Portrait Gallery*.

44 Reverend Ebenezer Miller (1799–1857) and his family. Calotype photograph by D O Hill and Robert Adamson. *Scottish National Portrait Gallery*.

46 Robert, 1st Lord Napier of Magdala (1810–1890). Oil painting by Michael Angelo Pittatore; probably after a photograph. *Scottish National Portrait Gallery*.

47 King Theodore II of Abyssinia (1818–1868). Carte-de-visite by Neurdein of Paris, about 1868. *Scottish National Portrait Gallery*.

49 Dejatch Alamayou, son of King Theodore II of Abyssinia (1861–1879). Photograph taken by the Royal Engineers at Ashangi, 1868, and included in an album of photographs by Ronald Leslie Melville, later 11th Earl of Leven. *Scottish National Portrait Gallery*.

50 British troops posing by the Kafir Bur Gate at Magdala, 1868. Collodion photograph probably taken by the Royal Engineers and inserted in an album of photographs by Ronald Leslie Melville, 11th Earl of Leven. *Scottish National Portrait Gallery*.

50 Prisoners in the stocks at Senafé, April 1868. Signed collodion print from an album of photographs, mainly by Ronald Leslie Melville, 11th Earl of Leven. *Scottish National Portrait Gallery*.

54 General Charles George Gordon (1833–1885). Mezzotint after a painting by Lowes Cato Dickinson. *Scottish National Portrait Gallery*.

55 *The death of General Gordon, Khartoum, 26th January, 1885*. Oil painting by George William Joy, exhibited in 1894. *Location unknown*.

55 Advertisement for Eno's Fruit Salts in *The Illustrated London News*, 8 August 1885.

59 Gilbert Elliott, 1st Earl of Minto (1751–1814). Oil painting by George Chinnery, 1812/13. *Scottish National Portrait Gallery* (PG L301, *on loan from Roxburgh District Council*).

61 General Sir David Baird (1757–1829). Oil painting by Sir David Wilkie, 1838; sketch for *Sir David Baird discovering the body of Sultaun Tippoo Sahib*. *Scottish National Portrait Gallery* (PG 644).

62 *Sir David Baird discovering the body of Sultaun Tippoo Sahib*. Oil painting by Sir David Wilkie, exhibited in 1839. *Private collection*.

63 Tipu's Tiger, the Man-Tiger-Organ. *Victoria and Albert Museum*.

64 *Die Seele*. Oil painting by Jan Balet. *Städtische Galerie im Lenbachhaus, Munich*.

65 Sir John Malcolm (1769–1833). Chalk drawing by William Bewick, 1824. *Scottish National Portrait Gallery* (PG 1051).

66 Henry Dundas, 1st Viscount Melville (1762–1811). Oil painting by John Rising; probably a version of the portrait exhibited in 1809. *Scottish National Portrait Gallery* (PG L123, *on loan from the Duke of Buccleuch and Queensberry*).

68 General Sir Charles James Napier (1782–1853). Bronze bust by George Gamon Adams, about 1853. *Scottish National Portrait Gallery* (PG 586).

69 General Sir Charles James Napier (1782–1853). *Kicking up a dust*, watercolour by unknown artist. *Private collection*.

70 James Ramsay, 1st Marquess of Dalhousie (1812–1860). Oil painting by Sir John Watson Gordon. *Scottish National Portrait Gallery* (PG 1119).

71 Maharajah Duleep Singh (1838–1893). Carte-de-visite photograph by Mayall of London. *Scottish National Portrait Gallery*.

72 Colonel Alexander Gardner (about 1801–1877). Photogravure; frontispiece to his *Memoirs* (London 1898). *Scottish National Portrait Gallery*.

75 Reverend Alexander Duff (1806–1878). Oil painting by John Faed, 1851. *The Church of Scotland*.

76 Reverend John Wilson (1804–1875). Calotype photograph of Wilson in Palestinian dress by D O Hill and Robert Adamson. *Scottish National Portrait Gallery*.

78 Reverend Dhanjibhai Nauroji (1822–1908) with Reverend John Jaffray. Calotype photograph by D O Hill and Robert Adamson; study for the Disruption Picture. *Scottish National Portrait Gallery*.

79 Reverend Stephen Hislop (1817–1863). Calotype photograph by D O Hill and Robert Adamson, about 1843. *Scottish National Portrait Gallery*.

81 *The Relief of Lucknow*. Engraving after a painting by Thomas Jones Barker, about 1859. *India Office Library and Records*.

82 Sir Colin Campbell's troops posing among the ruins of the barracks held by General Wheeler at Cawnpore. Photograph by Felice Beato, 1858. *National Army Museum*.

84 General Sir James Hope Grant (1808–1875). Oil painting by Sir Francis Grant, 1853. *Scottish National Portrait Gallery* (PG 343).

85 Sir James Outram (1803–1863). Oil painting by Alfred Buxton, 1863; probably completed with the aid of photographs. *Scottish National Portrait Gallery* (PG 1480).

87 Sir Colin Campbell, Lord Clyde (1792–1863). Oil painting by Thomas Jones Barker, 1860. *Scottish National Portrait Gallery* (PG 284).

87 Sir William Mansfield, later Lord Sandhurst (1819–1876), with Sir Colin Campbell, Lord Clyde (1792–1863). Photograph by Felice Beato 1857/8; subtitled *Good news in despatches*. *National Army Museum*.

88 Queen Victoria and her Indian attendant at Frogmore. Photograph taken in 1891. *National Portrait Gallery*.

Printed in Scotland for Her Majesty's Stationery Office by MacLehose & Co. Ltd., Glasgow
Dd. 630472/4093   C30   6/81